WHERE TRUTH
AND
JUSTICE MEET

WHERE TRUTH AND JUSTICE MEET

Clive Calver

HODDER & STOUGHTON
LONDON SYDNEY AUCKLAND TORONTO

British Library Cataloguing in Publication Data

Calver, Clive
  Where truth and justice meet.
  Evangelistic work
  I. Title
  269'.2   BV3790

ISBN 0-340-41065-5

CONTENTS

1

NO ONE EVER TOLD ME WHO I AM!

The vast ballroom was packed with people. Each had come with a different expectation yet everyone knew that this was a time for celebration. To meet with God, to listen to his Word and sing his praises.

On the distant stage a strong Welsh voice asked a basic question. 'How many of you here are committed Christians? You love Jesus and seek to live in relationship with him under the direction and authority of the Bible?'

Almost every hand was raised in response, each wanting to affirm his or her Christian position. But then came another question.

'How many of you would admit to being an evangelical?'

Consternation and confusion reigned. Many were unsure what the question meant, and were uncertain as to what their response should be. The word was not unfamiliar, but its precise meaning was unclear. Some hands shot up in clear recognition of what they believed. Many wavered until about one in three had their hands in the air. Two out of three did not respond.

'But an evangelical is a person who has committed his or her life to Jesus Christ, seeking to live under his Lordship and authority, believing and accepting the Bible for what it says.'

A murmur spread through the hall. Relief, as uncertainty could be abandoned. Shame at initial ignorance. Surprise that the answer should be so simple and straightforward.

The problem lies in the fact that words go out of fashion. At the same time the truths for which they stand may remain intensely relevant. The word 'evangelical' has come in for more than its fair share of abuse, rejection and misinterpretation.

There are many people today who freely misuse the term. It is confused with theological extremism, an anti-charismatic stance, or simply with a bigoted attitude towards others. Now, an evangelical is as capable of these attitudes as the next person, but they are not, in any sense, essential requirements for evangelicalism!

These innuendoes and pejorative attitudes have just added to the confusion and have led many of us as evangelicals to say things which we have later regretted. It has been said that 'confession is good for the soul' and I have to admit to denying my own evangelical heritage. As a young evangelist I faced a critical question from a Free Church pastor and hotly replied, 'I'm not an evangelical.' The phase typified a trendy assumption in the 1970s. It was designed to endear to, and not alienate from, the many non-evangelicals at the meeting. But it was also untrue.

The pastor was horrified. He could see my denying the fundamental beliefs on which evangelicalism is based. It is a deep regret to me that he died shortly afterwards and I was never able to explain that the incident nagged away at me. Was I just confused by the 'spirit of the age' towards evangelicalism? Was I rejecting truth and becoming confused by all the connotations that I understood were now loaded on to the word evangelical?

My own personal pilgrimage on this point lasted for about two years. My doctrinal position was clear throughout that period. It was words and prejudices which had undermined my position – I had to get back to the truth. I needed to think through issues which I had deemed irrelevant and again view evangelicalism in its historical perspective.

Undermined

Sadly, I have come to recognise that many today are in the same quandary. We are assaulted by objections and questions which make it easier to call ourselves just 'Christians'.

Any other additional descriptive term seems redundant. In fact, four major criticisms have to be faced.

1. We are told that to call ourselves 'evangelical' Christians is to exhibit 'party spirit'.
2. We are accused of inventing a new, modern word to justify our own theological position.
3. We face the charge that a new denomination is being created.
4. We are offered the choice of being 'evangelical' or 'charismatic'.

But these arguments beg the real issue. They stem from wrong presuppositions. They view evangelicalism as a structural or denominational commitment and that is not the case. Evangelicalism represents a theological commitment.

The very word 'theology' is sufficient to frighten some people into resistance. Yet it comes from two Greek nouns – *theos* and *logos*. In simpler language theology gives 'a word about God'. What makes someone an evangelical is his or her theological conviction, not their 'party', 'stream' or denomination.

An evangelical is, at root, someone who first of all holds to the traditional credal doctrinal statements of the Church. He or she believes that Jesus is in fact the Son of God. That he did perform miracles, rose from the dead and through his crucifixion offered an atoning sacrifice for the sins of all who would put their faith and trust in him. A commitment to the Trinity of Father, Son and Holy Spirit as the Godhead apart from all other faiths and beliefs, a recognition of the coming return of Jesus Christ and the fellowship of all believers as the Church of Christ are fundamental to an evangelical position.

Evangelicals are 'people of the book'. They recognise Scripture as truth, and in the words of the Lausanne Covenant, 'without error in all that it affirms'. This divinely given authoritative word from God can be totally trusted. Evangelicals may have some internal differences over the exact meaning of words like 'infallible' and 'inerrant', but have little doubt over the words 'inspired' and 'authoritative'. Indeed, where differences do exist, they are concerned primarily with the exact emphasis of what Scripture means in its context, not with what it claims for itself. For evangelicals the fact that the Bible is God's absolute Word to mankind is beyond dispute. (For a more detailed treatment of what evangelicals believe about the Bible, see Ian Barclay – *He Gives His Word*, a companion volume in this series.)

But evangelicals are not just distinguished by their adherence to doctrinal or biblical truth. They recognise mankind as 'fallen', polluted by sin, given over to practices which are anti-God, and alienated from God by their own actions. Satan is viewed as a personal opponent whose claims on the lives of mankind were overthrown by Christ on the Cross.

It is to Jesus Christ alone that the evangelical looks for salvation. A 'pluralist' philosophy, which claims there are several routes through different faiths to God, is wholeheartedly rejected. For the evangelical, God is not encountered through Buddha, Confucius, transcendental meditation, or any means other than Jesus – while other faiths may convey good thoughts about God and man, Jesus is the only way to know God as Father and Lord.

We may wonder about the fate of those who have never heard of Jesus, but Paul clearly affirms that conscience and creation point in that self-same direction (Rom. 1:20; 2:15).

To the evangelical the Gospel is 'good news'. Jesus has died and taken on himself in his crucifixion the penalty for the sins of mankind. To those who ask his forgiveness and receive his life in them by his Holy Spirit come the certainties of rebirth. Guilt and the past are removed. Christ establishes his rule and reign in their lives. Now they are integrated into the family of God – the Church.

The presupposition of 'universalism' – that one day all will be saved – is wholeheartedly dismissed. The truth of the matter is viewed this way. For those who reject Christ's offer of salvation is the tragic expectation of eternity without God. For those who begin a new life in relationship with Christ on

earth there is the glorious hope that this is only the beginning
of a never-ending story.

Standing on solid ground

The root word evangelical was first used in the early Church
as the Latin adjective '*evangelicus*'. In the fourth century AD,
Augustine used it to declare that 'the blood of the Christians
is, as it were, the seed of the fruit of the Gospel' (*semen fructuum
evangeliconum*).

It is interesting to note that 'evangelism' in German means
'Gospel', and that during the Reformation, Martin Luther
was horrified that his followers were termed Lutherans. He
adopted the title 'evangelicals' and wrote in 1524, 'A truly
evangelical man *would* not run here and there, he *will* stick to
the truth to the end.' In 1525 he added, 'People are good
evangelicals as long as they hope that the message of the
Gospel will pasture and enrich them' (Luther, *Works*, Wei-
mer edition).

Another word in popular usage was 'reformed', but by the
eighteenth century the term 'evangelical' had become an
umbrella term for both Lutheran and Reformed congregations.

The first use of the term in England dates back at least as
far as John Wyclif in the fourteenth century. He was named
'doctor evangelicus', and at the time of his death, in 1384, he
left an unfinished work entitled *Opus Evangelicum*. The first
date for the English word which the *Oxford English Dictionary*
gives is 1532 when Sir Thomas More referred to 'those
evangelicalles' in his *The Confutacyon of Tindales's Answere*.

Archbishop Cranmer used the word and it eventually
became common parlance for the work of God associated
with the names Wesley and Whitfield, which became known
as the Great Evangelical Awakening.

While there are several examples of the misuse of the word
today, John Stott boldly affirms that these are only devia-
tions. He asserts that, 'The classic connotation of "evangelical" is bound up with a theology of the Gospel which goes

back to the Reformation, and indeed beyond the Reformation to the Bible itself' (*Christ the Controversialist*).

Two terms best summarise evangelical convictions. *Sola Fide! Sola Scriptura!* (Faith Alone! Scripture Alone!) These twin pillars represent the primary supportive principles of the evangelical position.

(a) *Sola Fide* – it is impossible to earn our way into God's favour through our own human efforts. It is only by God's grace shown in his crucified Son who took our punishment on himself that we can be forgiven. Justification comes only by faith in Christ and that alone constitutes the good news of how we can receive salvation.

(b) *Sola Scriptura* – The traditions of the Church may be wise in precedent or principle, but they do not convey divine authority. That inspired authority is given only to Scripture which as the Lausanne Covenant (1974) firmly states is 'without error in all that it affirms'.

Other essential doctrines, the Trinity, the deity of Christ, the person and work of the Holy Spirit and many more follow naturally from these basic principles. Therefore evangelicalism is a statement of 'sound doctrine' which may then be worked out in and through a whole variety of denominational persuasions.

Stuck to a stereotype?

Evangelicalism is no bland monolithic structure. Within a framework of many different emphases is embraced a bewildering variety of diverse forms of worship and service.

Alternative viewpoints exist on just about every subject apart from the basic doctrinal distinctives. Participation of women in ministry, the charismatic movement, disestablishment of the state church, new forms of worship, sociopolitical involvement, the moral agenda and many others. Each has its protagonists and its opponents along with just about every shade of opinion in between.

Some choose to remain in denominational structures with non-evangelicals. Others abhor that practice. Some concentrate involvement in para-church societies, others look only to the local church as God's vehicle to express his love and grace within society. All these are 'extra-perspectives'. At the end of the day there are very few who will deny that the bottom line of the bond which holds them together is their common evangelicalism. It is only when that is denied, ignored, or just forgotten, that a real problem emerges.

It is at this point that younger evangelicals have tended to encounter problems. In forgetting our roots we have lost touch with the safeguards of basic belief. It is easy to forget that the Children of God sect, among others, started out from an evangelical stable, lost touch with their heritage, and fell into tragic error and excess.

It has become an easy practice in our culture to despise the past and affirm our individuality. It will take an openness to God's Spirit for evangelicals today to recover their sense of a common bond with each other. The alternative is to cut loose from our moorings and venture out on an uncommissioned voyage in uncharted seas. We reject our roots at our own risk!

2

SWIMMING AGAINST THE TIDE

There can be little doubt that the nineteenth century represented the heyday of evangelicalism. Churches were large and often filled with people. Parliamentary reforms were carried through by evangelical pressure to remedy working conditions for women and children. Social conditions were changed as the result of the campaigning zeal of leading evangelicals. Preachers drew crowds far greater than the theatres, and missionary activities became a burgeoning industry. The future looked full of promise.

Events in the mid-nineteenth century initiated the turning of the tide. The researches of Charles Darwin, coupled with the growing confidence of critical biblical scholarship, dealt body blows to the Church. Confidence and hope were eroded on the battlefields of the Somme to be replaced by scepticism and despair.

Through the twentieth century a steady exodus has taken place as people have left the churches. Secular humanism has quietly replaced a nominal Christian faith. Standards and attitudes have changed so that it has become highly unfashionable to be an evangelical in the 1980s.

We live in a society which is in rapid motion. All is in a state of flux. Today's generation loves to shake and question traditional values. The unusual and innovative come under the microscope of popular opinion – orthodoxy is deemed scarcely to merit a second glance.

It has always been difficult to generate enthusiasm for 'sound doctrine'. The fact remains that the swelling tide of secularism is making the task of defending the truth appear to be less and less enviable and more and more demanding.

When Channel 4 produced a series of programmes called 'Jesus – The Evidence', which dismissed traditionally-held opinions about the person of Jesus, the Evangelical Alliance mustered no less than forty-one theologians to protest about the inaccuracy of the scholarship involved in the programme.

Channel 4's reaction to this response was to broadcast the programmes and then to reveal their own reaction as, 'The powerful Evangelical Alliance viewed the series as a satanic enterprise with no redeeming features.' It is disturbing to note the reluctance to treat dissenting scholarship seriously.

Truth is increasingly viewed as being relative, and absolutes are dismissed. One might be excused for believing that the value of scholarship appears to be registered on a Richter scale according to the degree in which it creates an earthquake within traditional opinion. The higher the level of outrageousness of the latest theory, the greater its exposure to the maximum audience.

While the emphasis of modern marketing techniques is always to concentrate on the 'fashionable', 'new' or 'different', the value of the traditional and established becomes harder to maintain. Little credit is even given to being biblical; Scripture it seems is regarded as being of little value. At a time when 'accepted' positions face constant sceptical enquiry, experimental theology presents the media with a much more attractive proposition. Traditionally-held creeds or doctrines attract little exposure on the airwaves.

The tide has turned – with a vengeance!

Rearguard action

Faced with such a serious situation one might expect that evangelicals would have launched a spirited response. Such has sadly not been the case. It is almost as if the preacher's adage was employed by society – 'Case is weakest here – shout loudly!' Instead of a confident reply the Church responded with silence.

Sometimes bold statements can win a battle outright. In many ways that was exactly what happened. There were several skirmishes, but contemporary thinkers have gained the upper hand and are popularly believed to have had the Church 'on the run' ever since!

Having failed to win recognition or respect in the popular market-place, evangelicalism has quietly retreated into its own comfortable ghetto. There are, of course, notable exceptions, but, generally, the result has been divorce from the world at large.

The pressure points have emerged in four major areas of concentration:

1. *The challenge of science and technology* – the years since the industrial revolution have witnessed a major transformation in our society. Nowhere is this more evident than in the field of scientific and technological development.

   The major difficulty in responding to changes in this direction has not lain solely in countering the claims of science with Scripture – the main danger lies in the increasing tendency for modern technology to remove any sense of need for God.

   Imagine being in a modern-day fishing boat on the Sea of Galilee with the other disciples. Jesus lies asleep in the boat. A storm begins. What do you do? Wake Jesus? No, you'd probably start up the engine and head for the shore. There would appear to be no need to disturb Jesus.

   That is a vivid picture of the response of modern man. The new technological advances have removed the need for God. Why pray to God for help when you can rely on an outboard motor?

   This throws up a huge challenge as to how evangelicalism can respond to a society which no longer recognises a need for God.

2. *The challenge of rationalism* – the standard response to talk of God is now to question his existence. How do we know God is there? How can you be certain he is with you? How

do you prove Jesus rose from the dead? You hear his voice, what is it like? Questions abound, and all demand 'reasonable' answers.

The five senses dominate our thinking. If God is there then we must be able to perceive him with our senses; after all they provide the yardstick by which we judge all things!

It is at this point that most Christians will seek to draw on Scripture. We believe our certainties to be reasonable and well founded. They are based on God's word to us in the Bible. It is here that many will find the same retort from the world that has existed since the beginning of time. 'Did God really say' (Gen. 3:1). The new thinkers view Scripture, not as God's message to mankind, but as man's book about God. This distinction has proved to be very important indeed.

3. *The challenge of liberal theology* – it has often been noted that through the centuries the greatest damage to the Church has never come from outside but always from the enemy within.

Current wisdom would have us believe that because the Bible was written by men and women it was a purely human production. It is argued that biblical writers were not impartial about the matters of which they wrote and therefore display frequent natural bias. In other words, Scripture is not viewed in terms of objective fact, history or truth: it is seen as the record of events as filtered through the memory and perception of the biblical writers. They have, therefore, handed down to us the significance of the events as they saw them.

This point of view does not suggest that the Bible lies. It argues that the Gospel writers knew that Jesus was the Son of God so they simply interpreted events to give substance to their claims. We therefore have a book made up of saga, legend, myth, folklore and stories designed to help us view things in the same way as did the Early Church.

4. *The challenge of secularism* – it is here that the rubber hits the road! Belief in God ceases to be matter of importance; it descends to the level of personal preference. The argument is made that whether or not a Creator God set the wheels in motion, the universe is governed by natural laws. Day follows night, summer follows spring, an inexorable process. No immanent, ever-present God is seen as necessary because nature is viewed as the product of a closed-circuit mechanistic universe where one event naturally follows another.

Where does this lead? The secularist will argue that God, if there ever was a God, has absented himself. Therefore no miraculous happening can occur. No supernatural activity can disturb the pattern of natural order. Miracles become an invention designed to explain the unexpected. Life proceeds in an unending cycle.

This theory has devastating implications for an evangelical when it is applied to stories in the Bible. Take, for example, the feeding of the five thousand. If the miraculous is discounted, then Jesus is reduced to the level of a great moral teacher. His words, coupled with the action of the boy in surrendering his loaves and fishes provoked a similar response from the rest of the crowd who shared the contents of their previously hidden lunch-boxes with one another!

The result of this perspective is a view of history which provides the basis for biblical criticism. History is only an interpretation of events designed to fit into the presuppositions of the writer. Therefore, the German philosopher, Schleiermacher, announced in the eighteenth century, we can know little or nothing of the 'Jesus of history', all we can comprehend is the 'Christ of faith'. All we know of Jesus is how contemporary, and presumably biased, writers viewed him. They have their knowledge, not as objective reality, but as their own viewpoint. For us, therefore, our own response to the person of Christ is of far greater importance.

Once objective reality is dispensed with, personal preference becomes all important. Each person's concept of God provides its own self-authentication. God is only what you 'perceive him to be' as the Desiderata suggests. Each person has his own road to God. No absolute exists; each viewpoint, or religious faith, is equally valid to the individual believer.

Against this quartet of challenges, evangelicalism has been perceived as being in total retreat in the face of the onslaught. A belief in miracles, one God, a faith that defies proof, and a cosmology which flies in the face of science have become thoroughly *passé* in the eyes of a modern world.

Let battle recommence

The year of the Los Angeles Olympics was 1984. It was also the year of the Bishop of Durham. If British evangelicalism had to award a gold medal in that year it would surely have gone to the Rt Rev David Jenkins. His services to the cause of evangelical unity may have been unintentional, but they have certainly proved to be both timely and unique.

For years the 'ghetto' had served to insulate evangelicals from too much direct involvement in the secular debate. Many were totally unaware of the issues. It was the Bishop of Durham, in giving voice to his support of the concepts outlined previously, who rewrote the agenda and created the demand for an evangelical response.

Suddenly the talking-point in evangelical circles shifted from questions as to how high arms should be raised in worship or whether 'house churches' should be tolerated. Now real issues were aired, 'Was Jesus Son of God?' 'Were the miracles true?' and 'Could the Bible be trusted?'

For years the evangelical appeal had concentrated on the claims of simple faith. It appeared that the intellectual battle had been given up as lost. So, whatever reason might dictate, the one way we could still validate our position was to cling to the importance of personal experience. When all else failed, we could still sing,

You ask me how I know he lives?
He lives within my heart.

Instead of expressing a clear evangelical theology, many
evangelists resort simply to sharing personal experience.
This was well accepted by many people – but then it is easy to
respond positively. After all, one man's experience makes no
demand on anyone else. If that experience, or encounter with
God, compares favourably with the route tried by someone
else then it might deserve a try! Is this the level to which the
Gospel has been reduced? Our society freely accepts that
'one man's meat is another man's poison'. What works for
one rarely works for another, but even if it does there is no
demand or absolute involved: each person is free to 'do his
own thing'.

The claims of Scripture leave no such freedom. Jesus
clearly stated, 'I am the way and the truth and the life. No
one comes to the Father except through me' (John 14:6).
Popular secularism sees no possibility of such an intolerant
statement being valid. Each must be left to her, or his, own
way. So a Christian's experience can have validity – but of
equal worth is any statement from the follower of another
faith.

Now I am not attempting to pour cold water on the value
of personal testimony, but our statement of the Gospel needs
more content than individual experience alone. In reducing
the Gospel to that level we have accepted the lie of society
that no truth is absolute and there is no one saviour for
mankind.

For large sections of evangelicalism, recognition of the
problem dawned with the Bishop of Durham. When liberal
scholars were asked if they believed in the Resurrection the
answer would invariably be 'yes'. When asked if the tomb
was empty the answer would be 'no'. It was pure Schleiermacher – Christ had risen in the heart by faith, but the body
of Jesus remained incarcerated in the tomb.

Attempts to confine the debate to Anglican circles failed.
It was recognised that the principal of a Baptist theological

seminary had raised questions provoking similar concern only a few years earlier.

What was highlighted in the debate was the need for confident evangelical theological scholarship. Here light began to dawn! For years previously the number of evangelical ordinands at theological colleges had been increasing. Evangelical leaders, notably John Stott, had encouraged a new emphasis on evangelical scholarship in the face of science and philosophical criticism. The London Institute for Contemporary Christianity had already begun its valuable contribution to encouraging the development of a Christian mind in the face of a secular society.

Magazines and periodicals like *Third Way*, *Anvil*, *Churchman* and the *Evangelical Quarterly* were addressing key issues. Evangelical theologians were listened to with greater interest and respect. Bible colleges had already noted for some years an upturn in numbers. Pleas could be heard for a whole new generation of evangelical theologians which replaced the old scornful comments about 'head-knowledge, not heart-truth'.

Leap in the dark

What difference was this making to people in the pews? It would be foolish to argue that everything has changed – but much has begun to be set in motion. For years people had been told that it was absurd to believe that the Bible could be true. Scholars had 'proved' that it wasn't! At last a counter-cry was being raised – faith no longer had to be 'blind ignorance' – a raising of morale could clearly be discerned.

1. In certain quarters evangelical festivals and conferences had concentrated on the celebration of joyful experience. Now a new emphasis developed on sharing the content and application of faith.
2. A new emphasis is emerging on apologetics. It has been recognised that while liberal scholars were arguing that the Bible is built on man-made presuppositions unattested by truth, they lay themselves open to the very same charge.

While Christianity has hidden itself from science the fact remains that many scientists are also confident, committed Christians. Increasingly a response is vocalised to the challenge posed by our generation.

3. Many had been taught that faith must be blind. Evangelism in the 1960s often concentrated on encouraging people to 'try Jesus' through a blind leap of faith. Lapel stickers boldly announced, 'Turn on to Jesus'. Such a Gospel proved sadly deficient. Faith could not be proved by reason but nor was it independent of facts. Religion is not mere feeling. True faith is dependence on a God who has revealed himself in his Son and his Word. Here we have adequate ground for trusting ourselves to his mercy.

If all content is removed from the Gospel then Christianity is reduced to the level of an alternative mysticism, fitting for an Eastern guru, but scarcely worthy of the Living God.

A new emphasis on a thinking faith has provided the backdrop for the re-emergence of a strong, resurgent evangelicalism. There is evidence that, at long last, the twentieth-century fire of battle has produced regained nerve and a vibrant faith capable of recovering its rightful place in history.

3

SPEAKING GOOD NEWS

He stood alone.

One man in the middle of a crowd of tens of thousands. Yet the raised platform pointed the focus of national attention on to the lone individual.

One man, a big, black volume in his hand and the confidence to announce in a broad American accent that, 'the Bible says'. As hundreds of people streamed forward in response to his invitation to receive counsel and guidance for their spiritual lives something tugged at the heartbeat of a nation.

A largely hostile press began to review its opinions. While cynics sneered, ordinary men and women voted with their feet as they travelled to listen to a preacher. The challenge of the Christian faith provoked a response. Casual, everyday conversations turned to this man and his message. Weeks of crusade evangelism turned into months. Coaches converged on the capital bringing casual observers and committed devotees alike, from all parts of the country, to hear the message. TV and radio awoke to the fact that something was happening.

Churches stirred to a new sense of excitement. Could a genuine revival of spiritual interest be just around the corner? The crusade concluded in a blaze of publicity. The American and his team caught a plane home. It was over. But 1954 had changed the face of evangelicalism in Britain. A sense of frustration had been replaced by an overwhelming recognition of hope – and in that respect 1954 represented a watershed for evangelicals in Britain.

Fifty years of crisis

It is much too easy to see Britain as a 'Christian country' until the twentieth century. That has never been true. The Church and the Gospel have always endured peaks and troughs in terms of public interest. But, it is true that in 1851 the census revealed that more than half the population did, at least, attend church. Christian values affected moral and political issues alike. Christian truth was readily proclaimed, even though for many its acceptance was only nominal.

In the twentieth century this changed. Whether on the battlefields of the Somme or in the inequalities of national society, faith was eroded.

Sociologists pointed to the development of religion as an expression of society and a crutch for the needy.

Scientists scoffed at a Creator as evolution gained wider acceptance.

Philosophers saw miracles as a product of man's imagination and God as an 'absentee landlord'. If he had once existed, or not, at least we now knew that he had left this world to fend for itself.

Theologians acquainted the public with their general mood of scepticism about the Bible as representing historical fact or absolute truth.

This, coupled with man's inhumanity to man, demonstrated in two world wars, made the Christian faith an unpopular creed once the battlefields had been left behind.

It is true to say that these changes developed silent and unseen beneath the surface. The fabric of belief was retained. Churches and clergy still received respect. But beliefs, strongly expressed, were viewed as antiquated and outmoded. In the light of these pressures the Church subtly changed to bring itself into line.

Evangelicalism was viewed increasingly as a 'part' within the Church. It had always been that way, but now the lines were more clearly drawn. Strong in their confidence in Scripture, biblical doctrine and certain in the knowledge of Jesus as God's Son, dwelling in their lives, it was easy for evangelicals increasingly to withdraw into themselves.

Some saw God's call on them as a demand to be a 'faithful remnant'. Numbers were relatively unimportant. Doctrinal purity was vital. Evangelical churches existed to be the repository for divine truth available to any who would recognise it. There was an active hope that Christ would soon return. These were highly commendable desires, but the net result was, only too often, that evangelicals dug in for safety and sought to conserve their gains.

Others anticipated a mighty revival which would turn the tide. There was much prayer to this end. The 1850s had seen the second Evangelical Awakening. The campaigns of D. L. Moody had brought great blessing. The growth of the Keswick movement challenged Christians to be ready for what God could do. Then the 1904–5 Welsh Revival fanned these flames of hope. It sent reverberations around the world. Yet in Britain the flame flickered somewhat fitfully!

Fifty years later evangelicals in Britain were still actively working in evangelism through churches and evangelists alike. But decreasing church attendance in an expanding population was proving to be an accurate barometer of spiritual decline. No new initiative seemed capable of stemming the decline. Evangelical people were still waiting for something to happen.

New recruit to the army

God often uses his entrepreneurs. Strongly motivated individuals who ignore the spiritual carnage around them and get on with the job. Between the wars new Pentecostal churches were planted and saw numerical increase from the ministry of evangelists like the Jefferys brothers. After the Second World War Tom Rees hired the Royal Albert Hall on a regular basis for evangelistic meetings.

There always existed a small army of faithful witnesses committed to the proclamation of good news to the nation. Many worked away quietly in their own locality, church or denomination. Unsung heroes who just got on with things.

National Young Life Campaign, Youth for Christ, Campaigners, Crusaders, Covenanters and others provided a starting-point for many evangelists. They also offered an inter-denominational context for hearing the Christian message. Special-interest groups predominated on the evangelistic scene. There were missions to seamen, fishermen, servicemen, for village evangelism, to the down-and-out and many others. Groups as diverse as Counties Evangelistic Work, the various city missions and the London Embankment Mission all give the lie to any idea that nothing was being done. It was, but whether in local churches or national societies, evangelism was viewed as the province of a few specialists beavering away. It was the strident tones of Billy Graham echoing around Harringay Arena which placed evangelism firmly back on the ecclesiastical map!

The impact was fourfold:

(i) The sheer number and variety of new converts.
(ii) A return to confidence in simple, biblical preaching.
(iii) A regaining of morale within the local church.
(iv) An inspirational example to follow.

A sudden onrush of mini-Billy-Grahams was inevitable, but as evangelistic ministries matured they filled a vital gap in many local situations. Churches which had been suspicious of evangelistic enthusiasm and endeavour now began to take advantage of new opportunities. Church members found new opportunities for prayer and witness linked to local church evangelistic campaigns conducted by national evangelists.

The army was getting larger! What is more, evangelists themselves were proving to be the best recruiting officers. Many took on new, younger workers as apprentice or associate evangelists. Others began to lead teams. Numbers grew as new areas of evangelism began to open up. The Evangelists Conference, which owed its small beginnings to a handful of committed full-time workers in the 1960s, now attracts an annual attendance of around 300! Reliable estimates confirm that Britain now has several hundred full-time evangelists – and the number is still growing.

National or local?

It was not just by example that the visit of Billy Graham
helped to turn the tide for evangelism in Britain. Those few
weeks helped to restore morale. A sense of hope was created,
not just in the evangelist, but also in the message.

Thirty years later Mission England was to uncover large
numbers of clergy and evangelical leaders around the country who had been converted at Harringay. They hadn't left it
there! Churches were greatly encouraged by the reinforce-
ments. Evangelical Bible schools and theological colleges
were growing in size and number. Books were written and
magazines produced. The future looked bright, but beneath
the surface things were not so promising. The opportunities
were there, but leadership and strategy were at a premium.

Individual initiatives went well. 'Bash' Nash was leading
young men from public schools to Christ in his famous camps
and grooming and encouraging them to future leadership.
Lindsay Glegg was adding impetus and strength to the
Movement for World Evangelisation and 'Filey Week'. But
with the solitary exception of the year 1955, church attendance went on declining. The Indian summer was over.

Two solutions offered themselves. One was to develop new
strategies for evangelism within the local church. The other
was to look again at what had already worked so well. Bring
Billy back. Tragically British evangelicals have often displayed a reluctance to get involved personally in evangelism.
So often the cry has gone out for the professional.

The next twelve years saw three more London crusades
along with Scottish, Northern Ireland and Northern England crusades conducted by the Graham team. Results were
encouraging, thousands were converted – but was this really
the way forward?

Seventeen years on

Billy was back. This time the package was to be very different. Training programmes, nurture groups to conduct

follow-through of interest from the mission, prayer triplets – these all brought their own distinctive flavour and spoke of lessons learned over the seventeen-year period. Coupled with these innovations and particularly emphasised by Mission to London, where Luis Palau was the major evangelist, was a large number of local evangelistic campaigns conducted mainly by British evangelists.

Within the changes could be read a renewed commitment to personal witness, prayer and localised evangelism yet with a major emphasis on the national campaign as a focal point for media interest. The results were spectacular. Over 1,000,000 people attended the two missions and over 100,000 made a personal response to the preaching of the Word of God. Mission Sheffield and Mission Solent were to evoke a similar response.

The turning tide

The tide of evangelism now ran high. Long-term evangelistic ministries of men like Dick Saunders, Don Summers, Tony Stone, Ron Spillards and Don Double had paved the way for a growing number of evangelists. The 1970s were to see a growing attendance at the annual Evangelists Conference. The formation of the Christian ministries team which combined the involvement of John Blanchard, Peter Anderson and Derek Cleave was to give a clear-cut 'reformed' evangelistic thrust through missions in a number of local churches.

The newspaper *Evangelism Today* was to provide a helpful service in sharing news of what was happening in evangelism around the country.

Meanwhile, evangelism was becoming a vital ingredient in the activity of 'charismatic' churches. Initial fears of a disregard for outreach amid the spontaneous joy of new-found freedom in worship began to be dispelled as new evangelistic initiatives began in the early 1970s, notably those beginning from the ministry of David Watson at St Michael-le-Belfry in York.

Celebration became a facet of many town and city-wide

missions. Drama and dance were to join music in playing a part in a multifaceted presentation of the Gospel. Some also introduced an emphasis on healing, 'signs and wonders', and a challenge to the forces of occultism and drug addiction.

Teamwork in evangelism, mobilising the local church for mission, became a feature which Manna Ministries today carries on in its initiation of local church urban campaigns. Church planting in the inner city became the focal concern of the Ichthus team headed by Roger and Faith Forster.

Co-operation was becoming a keynote. Gavin Reid returned from his outstanding contribution to Mission England to encourage a team of evangelists at the Church Pastoral Aid Society. The Saltmine Trust became a major national force with Dave Pope, Doug Barnett and Ian Coffey joining forces. Independent evangelists, like Eric Delve, were drawing growing crowds. A new wave of evangelism was building on the old foundations – alongside the well known was a veritable army of workers quietly getting on with the job of pioneering means to tell others about Jesus.

These developments were being paralleled in the ministry of local churches. Two new words were added to the vocabulary of church life; 'church growth' had arrived. Introduced and encouraged by the influential Bible Society, Tom Houston, Eddie Gibbs and Roy Pointer along with Monica Hill first at the Evangelical Alliance and then through the British Church Growth Association. The impetus continues today. Churches have begun to plan for growth. New emphasis is placed on the role of small groups or 'cells' in evangelism. The patterns of local church life are seen as central and the commitment of members to personal witness is viewed as vital for growth. For many churches this has marked a significant new beginning in encouraging 'every-members ministry'.

With this weight of new activity one might be entitled to ask whether Britain is now evangelised. The fact remains that the task is huge and the downward trend in church attendance had been a fact of life for decades. The Marc Europe and Evangelical Alliance report, 'Beyond the Churches', focused attention on the huge variety of 'people groups' unreached by the churches in today's society. New initiatives have certainly helped to stem the decline. Advances in evangelism have begun.

One-to-one personal witness, trans-denominational co-operation in evangelistic efforts, grass-roots evangelism in schools, youth clubs, at the factory floor and at the school gate, all these have proved to represent the new tide of evangelistic initiatives in Britain today.

A new morale is emerging, but question-marks do remain. The tide could be turning, but history alone will tell whether a major break-through is to be made before the close of the twentieth century.

Inner-city areas, ethnic groups, the villages of Britain all illustrate real ignorance of the Christian message. The classroom and the shop-floor tell the same story. But hope is in the air, expectancy is high and the army of witnesses is growing! Time will tell whether 1984 represented a significant turning-point, or a bump of encouragement on the long way down.

4

GETTING THEIR HANDS DIRTY!

'Evangelicals care only about souls.' They never really demonstrate a concern for the welfare of 'people'.

This post-war cliché represented a convenient battle-cry for liberal Christianity. It perpetuated the myth that while evangelicals proclaimed a gospel of words, the broader streams of churchmanship introduced the kingdom through action. Evangelicals could safely devote themselves to doctrinal concerns, meanwhile non-evangelicals tackled the key issues of the day.

Evangelicals, in turn, were bitterly opposed to the reduction of the Christian faith to the level of a club for those who wished to serve their fellow men. They saw the 'social gospel' as a very pale reflection of the message of life and hope for eternity which Jesus came to bring. They were distressed to see the Cross reduced to the level of a symbol of love and obedience. Notions of sin and forgiveness seemed excluded.

The 'social gospel' seemed only to address the human needs of today. By contrast, evangelicals looked to a message which provided security for life beyond the grave. These two creeds developed as 'either . . . or' positions. Few were persuaded that they needed to be wedded.

It all hinged on a view of man. 'Liberal' Christians possessed huge confidence in man and could dream of building Utopia, which was equated with the kingdom of God, on earth. Evangelicals were more gloomy about man's capacity to do good. Social action was therefore viewed as a waste of time and social transformation as completely impossible. They concentrated their efforts, at the start of the twentieth century, on anticipating Christ's return. This was the only true hope for mankind.

The findings of one American sociologist have been summarised in these words:

> The general picture that emerged from the results presented . . . is that those who place a high value on *salvation* are conservative, anxious to maintain the *status quo* and unsympathetic or indifferent to the plight of the black and the poor . . . Considered all together, the data tends to suggest a portrait of the religious-minded as a person having a self-centred preoccupation with saving his own soul, an other-worldly orientation, coupled with an indifference toward, or even a tacit endorsement of, a social system that would perpetuate social inequality and injustice (David O. Moberg, *The Great Reversal*).

Danger, triumphalism at work

He was the principal of a major theological college. His brief that evening was quite straightforward. He had to address the Christian Union at a large university. Before speaking he sat through a lengthy period of worship. The theme was a simple one. The students sang with great gusto of their desire to regain the land for Jesus. They voiced their commitment to take back Satan's strongholds, to speak to the nation and to reclaim areas long since abandoned.

He determined to ask, with the long summer vacation only a few weeks ahead, what they were going to do. He asked for information about missions, projects, areas of Christian activism. How would they set about their task?

The tragedy lies in the fact that amid our high-sounding phrases and joyful singing little may actually happen to impinge on the society in which we live. Too often the right words are used as an inadequate substitute for right actions. Suburban comforts are too often valued above the real sacrifices entailed in being involved where it really hurts!

This kind of glib triumphalism is only too common.

Evangelicals have waited in vain for political solutions, or for the problems just to disappear. Ignoring the situation has not provided any answers. The need has arisen not for a new kind of evangelical, but one of an old type.

As many as 250 years ago the prospects for a change in the situation appeared similarly gloomy. It was on the Continent that the first ray of hope appeared. Count von Zinzendorf opened up his estate as a haven for Moravian refugees. A building named 'Herrnhut' – the Lord's house – was utilised. A prayer meeting began which was to continue uninterrupted for 100 years!

The events which followed were interconnected, though not directly related to a human strategy or agenda. Moravian missionaries were instrumental in leading John Wesley, among others, to a firm commitment to Jesus Christ. Wesley, Whitefield and many others traversed Britain on horseback preaching good news. Half the nation were to hear the Gospel in what historians have called 'the great Evangelical Awakening'. Some have boldly asserted that this factor, above all others, prevented Britain's enduring the bloody revolution which the French suffered.

Their spiritual children, grandchildren, and great-grandchildren were to make an enormous contribution to the general welfare of society. Orphanages were built, prison visits established, medical and nursing care advanced, Sunday schools established and a tradition begun of evangelical involvement in education.

On the political field, slavery was abolished, the hours and conditions of work for women and children radically altered by Acts of Parliament and policies of religious tolerance advanced.

Conditions in mental hospitals, child prostitution, criminal welfare, prison reform and child abuse were all issues which did not escape attention. In each area evangelicals were to play a major role in challenging the attitudes and very fabric of society. God's people saw the Gospel as affecting the whole of life, not just the souls of individual men and women.

The last thirty years have produced a 'harking-back' to those halcyon days.

An increasing desire has been generated to demonstrate the Gospel and to copy the example of Jesus Christ; this is leading to a radical commitment to share in the hurts and identify with the needs felt by our society. Indeed some have observed a 'great reversal' in evangelical attitudes and a genuine return to roots of social and political involvement.

As John Stott has aptly put it, 'Saving faith, and serving love belong together. Wherever one is absent, so is the other. Neither can exist in isolation' (John Stott, *Issues Facing Christians Today*, Marshalls, 1984).

Candle in the dark

The sobering recognition of the scale of the task has led to a proliferation of new evangelical initiatives. Societies have been formed and reports framed to combat a variety of social evils. Moral issues, urban deprivation, unemployment, overseas aid, support for the persecuted, drug abuse and racial tension among many other issues have all been addressed.

One essential need has been information and research. The Shaftesbury Project and the London Institute for Contemporary Christianity have distinguished themselves in this respect, particularly in regard to urban issues. On matters of moral concern the work of Care Trust has acted as an 'early warning system' for many.

In combating specific areas of concern a significant beginning was made. It is currently no more than a beginning, but represents an important break-through in targeting areas where evangelicals believe that a change in society is essential. Not all will always agree. But such 'unity in diversity' is probably the fundamental distinctive of evangelicalism!

The target gathering of those concerned over the drift into moral decline within this nation was the Festival of Light. It focused national attention on what the organisers perceived as the wholesale desertion of Christian values amid the flood of contemporary secularism. Out of this gathering was to develop the nationwide Festival of Light which was to grow into the twin-pronged initiatives of Care Trust and Care Campaigns. These bodies collate information, initiate campaigns (both within and outside Parliament), and provide constructive guidelines for positive Church action on moral issues like abortion, single-parent families and the bias perceived towards homosexual preference in community and educational services.

Some evangelicals have put their efforts behind Mary Whitehouse and her National Viewers' and Listeners' Association. Others have invested their energies in small but highly significant evangelical groups like True Freedom Trust, Turn About and Pilot. These have all been established in order to share the Christian message with those involved in the 'gay' community.

A commitment to reach people where they are, rather than where one would want them to be, has always clearly marked out the work of Frontier Youth Trust (FYT). This arm of Scripture Union exists to contact and help those young people who could not normally be contained within the normal youth outreach of the local church. In co-operation with the Evangelical Urban Training Project, In Contact Ministries, the Shaftesbury Project and Evangelical Christians for Racial Justice (formerly the Evangelical Race Relations Group), FYT has done a great deal to focus evangelical concern on areas of urban deprivation.

These five organisations together form the Evangelical Coalition for Urban Mission (ECUM). As such they seek to inform and cajole a realistic awareness in the largely 'suburban' ranks of evangelicalism of those major areas of need which exist in the inner city. High levels of unemployment, racial abuse, poverty, homelessness, violence, injustice and dwindling church congregations may well be facts of life. That, they would contend, does not give evangelicals the right to wash their hands of the situation. A strong cry has gone up from ECUM and others for evangelicals to return to the inner city. The need has been highlighted to redress areas

of discrimination and inequality within the church and to
address those abuses which exist outside it.

Some progress has been made in establishing drop-in
centres for the unemployed, community enterprise projects
and job creation schemes. These projects, normally operated
by groups of local churches, represent only a 'drop in the
bucket' when compared to the size of the problem. But they
do serve to show what can be done when Christians take their
responsibilities seriously.

Ministry to prisoners (Prison Christian Fellowship, David
Stillman Evangelistic Association and others), help for those
gripped by solvent or drug abuse (Yeldall Manor, Life for the
World, etc.), support for the mentally or physically handicapped (Torch Trust for the Blind, Deaf Christian Fellowship, Christian Concern for the Mentally Handicapped)
all speak of growing Christian initiatives. Page after page
could be filled with reports of such ventures, and many
others!

Youth clubs, camps, residential centres, hospital and
prison visitation programmes, help for the elderly, are in-
dicative of the rise in awareness within the local church that
Christian responsibility needs to be practical in its outwork-
ing.

The Salvation Army has always been in the forefront of
demonstrating Christian concern, and has therefore earned
respect for its message. One London city missionary told me
recently of the growing number of contacts he had with
non-Christians. This was because he and his wife used their
home as a distribution centre for furniture and household
utensils. These were passed to needy local people in a
particularly deprived area of one London borough. Having
received visible evidence of concern, local people were far
more ready to listen to 'good news'.

Whether in the village or the city, evangelicalism has
passed through hard times. Perhaps a salutary warning has
now been received that we need to regain the zeal of our
evangelical forefathers in addressing social issues before our
message will be readily received. After all, the Early Church

were only giving an explanation of their lifestyle in preaching the Gospel!

'Feed the hungry'

This injunction from Jesus is one which evangelicals have to take seriously. And hunger does not just come in one variety. It is to spiritual famine that our efforts have primarily been addressed.

Sunday schools, Bible classes and groups, books and magazines, church services and missions have concentrated energies on sharing the message about Jesus Christ. These activities have mainly been concentrated on those who would 'come to us'. They have also presumed on a high degree of literacy.

Concern about this situation has not been far beneath the surface. But it does represent a major challenge for evangelicalism today.

The days when TEAR (The Evangelical Alliance Relief) Fund was born will go down in the annals of evangelical history. Founded with a view to helping refugees or the victims of disaster, its annual income has risen from £50,000 in 1969 to over £10 million today.

While maintaining its original aims TEAR Fund has expanded its brief to the giving of development grants, support for evangelism and Christian education, individual sponsorship of children and students in developing countries, handicraft marketing and the sending of specially skilled personnel overseas. Today some eighty people are serving overseas and projects are being funded in almost seventy countries, all in conjunction with either local churches or other Christian agencies.

Other evangelicals have channelled support through World Vision, or through bodies representative of broader churchmanship like Christian Aid.

The black churches

The waves of immigration from the West Indies to England in the 1950s and 1960s suddenly precipitated thousands of established evangelical believers into church and parish alike.

Sadly, problems were not far behind.

It was not just a matter of skin colour which separated these new streams of believers from traditional evangelicalism; culture played its part.

One medical doctor has spoken of how he felt as a black man in 1950s Britain when children would rush on to the streets to view this new phenomenon.

The problems which confronted black believers were enormous. They included a very different form of worship, difficulties in obtaining acceptance and recognition and the pressures of non-evangelical churchmanship. The sad story which unfolded was to be one of missed opportunities and neglected responsibilities.

Today there are dozens of different groupings among black churches, with little interrelation. It can only be hoped that groups like Evangelical Christians for Racial Justice will help to remove areas of racial abuse. The emergence of the West Indian Evangelical Alliance (as part of the Evangelical Alliance) may well provide a much-needed bridge for black and white evangelical Christians to cross over and learn from each other.

Agreeing to differ

It would be surprising, and unfortunate, if all evangelicals held the same political opinions as each other. At least on the subject of challenging state authorities to cease persecution of evangelical believers, there is an inevitable unity. But on issues concerning the environment or on the matter of nuclear warfare there would be at least two sides in a debate among evangelicals.

The same divorce has been projected into the moral-social division.

Sadly, these areas have merely been viewed as complementary. It has often proved easier to isolate and concentrate on one or the other. This has, in turn, served to illustrate that evangelicals can be more readily roused to relatively 'painless' protest on matters of moral concern than to generate a positive response in areas of social evil.

More recently the Evangelical Alliance has sought to encourage a recognition of the vast range of activities conducted by member societies and of the essential unity which must exist between them. A morally-sick society will tolerate social injustice; to address the one issue must equally lead to a commitment to see change in the other. Only by taking to heart the wide range of separate agendas and determining to confront them all will Christians again assert their role as bringing light into the darkness.

It is clear that over 1,000,000 evangelical believers form a significant force. It is also apparent that their political diversity protects them from being viewed as just a 'moral majority'. Greater co-operation between the various emphases of concern will enable Christians to grapple with a wider range of issues which overlap with each other. Then we may begin to fulfil the dreams of one evangelist who wrote to me in these words, 'It's not much, but it's better to light a candle than to grumble about the darkness.'

5

SEPARATED BRETHREN

The twentieth century has been hailed as 'the era of Christian unity'. Divisions which have existed for centuries are being broken down. Alliances, mergers and unions are creating new opportunities for a united voice. 'Co-operation' is the catch-word of the age.

Nowhere is this more clearly seen than in the creation, after the Second World War, of the World Council of Churches and its British equivalent (the BCC). Through these bodies a vehicle now exists for transdenominational, international co-operation. With these agencies ecumenical partnership became a reality.

The tangible results are impressive. Aid programmes and relief ventures have been launched in famine-stricken areas; support has been given to ethnic minorities; partnerships in mission schemes have been launched; dialogue has been established with those of other faiths; and plans launched to encourage the evangelisation of Britain.

Although prospects of union between Anglicans and Methodists have for the moment been shelved, the United Reformed Church has been born out of a merger of Presbyterian and Congregational Churches and serious discussions are taking place about the relationship between the Anglican and Roman Catholic communions.

Dialogue, friendship and partnership have become normal. One cannot but applaud the desire to see Christ's prayer in John 17:11, 'that they may be as one', fulfilled in our generation.

The only problem is – at what cost to doctrine?

Present initiatives appear highly commendable to the casual onlooker. Without seeking to be too critical we must ask if they are really practical. The arguments are coherent and plausible – but how do evangelicals evaluate the results?

Ecumenism

Here we must firmly grasp the nettle of the basic issue. If all denominations and churches are welded together, does that fulfil Christ's desire? Would the result of such a union constitute the true Church?

To become still more controversial in our search for an honest appraisal, we must ask: does the Church of Christ include those who deny that he is the Son of God? Does it incorporate those who deny his miracles, bodily Resurrection or Virgin Birth? Can evangelicals seriously be expected to join hands with a Church which looks for its guidance to a man whose utterances on certain matters and in certain times are deemed to be infallible? Does the term 'Christian' rightly include those who deny the inspiration/infallibility of Scripture? Can we be 'all as one', if some consent to the traditional creeds of the Church while others deny them?

This may sound intolerant of the spirit of our age, but aren't there some things which are just not negotiable?

In the past when the great doctrines of the Church have become blurred, the whole of Church life has declined and in some cases ceased to exist altogether . . . In 1685 in north-west China at a place called Sianfu, evidence was discovered of the existence of a church in China in the seventh and eighth centuries . . . The evidence was on a stone . . . it shows . . . that the Christians in eighth-century China adjusted their doctrine to accommodate the views of the Chinese intelligentsia . . . They wanted to win the Chinese Buddhist and Confucianist, and because the death and resurrection of Christ was such a stumbling block they toned down their teaching . . . instead of winning the educated Chinese, the Christian Church vanished without trace (Ian Barclay, *The Facts of the Matter*, Falcon, 1971).

Here we stand

British evangelicalism has a forceful independent streak. Since the Reformation, whenever the Gospel is felt to be threatened, evangelicals have demonstrated their dissent. The Puritans, Wesley and Methodists, Charles Spurgeon within the Baptists, the emergence of the Brethren – all speak of a tendency to disassociate from doctrinal compromise or error.

The strong commitment of evangelicals to a bold and fearless proclamation of the Gospel has induced a similar fear of being too closely linked with institutional Christianity. Where the message is compromised, or kept under cover, then evangelicals will always consider secession. It is, therefore, not surprising that this tradition has continued in the twentieth century.

A strong and vociferous body of evangelical opinion has urged evangelical non-co-operation with the forces of ecumenism. Five main reasons have been given:

1. Guilt by association. If evangelicals join with non-evangelicals then our witness is tarnished and the world is confused as to what Christianity is really about.
2. Oil and water never mix! The forces of unbelief and sceptical criticism can never be joined to those who hold to the Bible as God's Word to mankind. Too often the ecumenical movement seems to be only papering over the cracks of fundamental areas of disagreement.
3. The World Council of Churches donates money to all kinds of causes including guerrilla activities in certain countries.
4. Uniformity is never God's purpose. It is the best that man-made union can hope to achieve. The danger comes when the ground of our unity is formed on the basis of our agreement to the lowest common denominator. Therefore

our position on the Gospel, Scripture and basic doctrinal viewpoints would be constantly undermined.

5. The Church is Christ's body, the Gospel his message, therefore we must not use the former as a political tool to compromise the latter in conversation with those of other faiths. We need to proclaim the good news to others, not determine its content in discussions with them.

Failure to be friends

Sadly these views have not always been expressed in the most gracious or tactful manner. It has been easy to accuse evangelicals of being 'bigoted' or 'hardline'. Often this has prevented non-evangelicals from appreciating the full force of evangelical difficulties with ecumenism.

Widespread pleas for unity have placed many evangelicals in a difficult position. They have felt pressurised. This particularly applies to those who are involved in 'mixed' denominations (i.e., denominations which contain both evangelicals and non-evangelicals). On the one hand their very denominational affiliation commits them to a degree of ecumenical co-operation, on the other they see real value in acting as 'salt and light', standing for truth within the denomination.

Often the issue has been polarised into two standpoints. 'Come out' and retain doctrinal purity in fellowship with fellow evangelicals. 'Stay in' and retain influence in the corridors of national and denominational power. That way a great deal of good can be done and real influence obtained, but at the cost of suspicion and criticism from fellow evangelicals. The choice is not an easy one and evangelicals have been drawn both ways.

The fact is that while conclusions have differed, right motives have generally applied. Some, like Michael Harper, have felt that 'the new ecumenism essentially trusts in the Holy Spirit to guide and lead into all truth. It believes that Christian love initiates, and that we need to have our prejudices and fears removed so that we can take that initiative'

(*Three Sisters*, Tyndale House, 1979). For that reason they have endeavoured to contribute true evangelical concepts into the ecumenical framework. Others have felt that only compromise on fundamental issues could result, and that would be much too high a price to pay.

Tragically, the result has too often been to create hostility between evangelicals, rather than an openness to allow each to follow his own conviction on the matter. While some have come closer to non-evangelicals, others have separated themselves from their fellow evangelicals. The result has not been unity but schism.

The great divide

In 1966 at the National Assembly of Evangelicals, sponsored by the Evangelical Alliance, Dr Martyn Lloyd-Jones issued a challenge to evangelicals to separate themselves by coming out of mixed denominations. John Stott, who chaired the meeting, felt that he had to voice his disagreement.

Since then two movements have run in parallel:

1. Anglican evangelicals have greatly strengthened their links with each other and emphasised their denominational loyalty. Two major National Evangelical Anglican Congresses at Keele and Nottingham have laid down firm foundations. The Church of England Evangelical Council and the annual Anglican Evangelical Assembly have provided the means for debate and decision on key national issues affecting evangelical Anglicans. Their local counterpart has been provided by diocesan evangelical fellowships.

The Eclectics group acts as a meeting-point for the under-40s as does the Senior Evangelical Anglican Conference for their older counterparts. The *Church of England Newspaper* acts as a major source of news and views relevant to these groupings. The differing viewpoints of evangelical Anglicans have meant that they are served by two theological journals – *Anvil* and *Churchman*. It would be a mistake to assign too strong a degree of homogeneity to the views of Anglican evangelicals, but within their diversity has come a strong degree of denominational unity.

One significant wing of opinion is served by the Church Society which generally mobilises those who would hold to a Reformed theological opinion. On a broader base the Church Pastoral Aid Society conducts a valuable supportive role towards local churches.

Through the Evangelical Group on General Synod, church policy can be affected and a further key change has been in the number of evangelicals serving as bishops, archdeacons, rural deans and in other positions of influence. In only twenty years the pendulum has swung to such an extent that the majority of Anglican ordinands now emerge from evangelical colleges. For evangelicals in general that represents good news!

2. On the other side of the fence things are vastly different. Free Church evangelicals who responded to the lead of Dr Lloyd-Jones have rooted their energies firmly within the context of the local church. The Westminster Fellowship acts as a fraternal base for occasional contact and study together. The British Evangelical Council provides a means of addressing national issues.

Small denominational groupings such as the Strict Baptists, or the larger Fellowship of Independent Evangelical Churches provide a structure into which local autonomous or semi-autonomous churches can relate in loose association. A reformed evangelical theological position is fairly uniform in the 1,300 or so churches which fall into this category.

The foundation of a conference for Reformed charismatics indicates an interesting development in these circles. Different emphases within this group are served by two major newspapers – *Evangelicals Now* and *Evangelical Times*.

Building bridges

For over 120 years the disparate and diverse ranks of British evangelicals had found common voice in the Evangelical

Alliance. The 1966 debate brought that fundamental unity into serious question. A link which had been, at best, tenuous was placed under extreme pressure.

Pentecostals, Baptists, Methodists and the Brethren assemblies which were in membership with the Alliance tended to continue as if nothing had happened. Free Church evangelicals, who leaned towards a 'separatist' position, withdrew to concentrate their efforts on uniting only with those who stood outside 'mixed denominations' through the organ of the British Evangelical Council.

Anglicans, meanwhile, rejuvenated by the Keele Congress and stirred to a major assault within the denomination, retained their links within the Alliance, although perhaps on a more nominal basis than before.

Within ten years it could be said that while many Anglicans viewed the Alliance as a Free Church enterprise, an equivalent number of Free Churchmen viewed it as an Anglican 'front' organisation. The year 1966 had served to polarise evangelicals into positions of alienation and often mutual mistrust.

Recent years have provided some evidence of a growing desire to understand one another. It would be wrong to speak of a 'change of heart'; what appears to be emerging is a greater respect for the integrity of those who hold to each position. The challenge of a largely pagan society has served to evoke mutual recognition of the importance of standing together. Coupled with the need for a common voice to withstand the vocal forces of liberal theology this presents cogent arguments for a change in the divided state of evangelicalism.

Old wounds heal slowly. Time will tell whether evangelicals can find common cause together again, while retaining their own individual distinctives. However, the old cry of 'unity in diversity' is being heard, and signs point to a changing situation:

- Consultations between evangelical leaders.
- Co-operation in resisting change in the laws governing Sunday trading.

– Rapidly escalating membership figures within the Evangelical Alliance.
– Over 1,500 evangelical leaders survive a week together at Leadership '84.

All these, and many more, point to the potential of new beginnings. As dialogue between evangelicals increases it can only be hoped that differences will diminish and the opportunities to learn from one another will be seized. The grace to differ over non-essentials in order to affirm basic unity will be vital. For the fact remains that evangelical disunity is as clear a denial of biblical truth as an ecumenical unity based on compromise towards fundamental truths. One cannot be discarded without the other's being sought.

In the eighteenth century Richard Baxter grappled with these issues, wisely concluding in words with a striking relevance for today:

> In things essential – unity;
> In things doubtful – liberty;
> In all things – charity.

6

LEARNING TO LIVE TOGETHER

Even the best-ordered households have disagreements, if
only occasionally. Most families manage to fall out among
themselves from time to time. New ideas, fresh ways of doing
things can create both tensions and division. Stubbornness
on both sides of an argument can create bitterness and hurt.
Some may decide to leave home, others are asked to go, but
usually the prodigal is welcomed back. Disagreements can
be forgiven, arguments forgotten, for family always remains
family.

So often this is a true picture of life within the Church.

The preceding chapter presented a cautionary tale, for
division is often seen as the simplest means of maintaining
one's own position.

The charismatic movement emerged within mainline denominational churches during the 1960s. It was not long
before some of its adherents were being asked to leave, and
others were opting out in sheer frustration. Family differences rose to the surface.

Churches were divided, new churches formed. Movements emerged on both sides of the divide. Friends found
they could no longer agree with each other; relationships
were severed; and respect was soured as anger and hurt
grew.

Only twenty years later evangelicals were united in
mourning the loss of David Watson, institutional non-
charismatic evangelical leaders spoke alongside new house-
church charismatic leaders, signifying that 'spot the
charismatic' had become yesterday's game.

At one major Christian festival it was possible to look along a line of worshippers. One raised arms in worship while his neighbour had his hands firmly earthed in his pockets. Another danced in worship while her neighbour bowed in silent meditation. A third lifted hands waist-high (at half-mast!) while alongside him a lady was hanging on to her hymn-book for survival! It spoke of unity in diversity, of variety in styles of worship, born in the same faith and offered to the same Lord.

It would be folly to suggest that conflict is no more. Too many have suffered from the words and actions of their brothers and sisters and have not been able to forget the hurt. Others are locked into a view of their positions as being totally correct, representing absolute truth. But all the indications are that the family is being reunited and that understanding and mutual tolerance will win the day.

Charismatic or evangelical?

It has become popular in some circles to draw a distinction between the two. It is argued that the charismatic emphasis emerged from a desire to see God's power displayed at work among his people. Conversely, evangelicals are depicted as a people content to rest in God's truth revealed in Scripture.

The problems of this approach are easy to see. Charismatics become, on this basis, a dangerous new development. On the one hand, they can be viewed as moving beyond Scripture by placing an undue emphasis on human experience. Alternatively, they appear as those who have moved beyond evangelicalism on to a higher plane where God is seen to be at work today.

Although the distinction sounds attractive, it lacks objectivity. If evangelicalism is not a mere party in the Church but speaks of a people committed to biblical truth, whatever their style of worship or form of Church government, then this distinction becomes totally artificial. An evangelical maintains that Jesus is the Son of God, the Bible is the inspired, infallible Word of God and that the traditional credal doctrinal statements of the Church are still the foundation of an evangelical position today. If a charismatic denies these basic doctrines which constitute an evangelical position, then we must accept that they are not evangelical. But we might also doubt that they properly represent a charismatic position.

There are plenty of counterfeits around. People who speak in tongues which are not from God; who practise healing within a context which fails to give Christ the glory; who prophesy that which is not in accordance with Scripture. Clearly these people are not evangelical, but are they charismatic either?

On the other hand, one must have the right to query the evangelical integrity of those who simply reject any possibility of a supernatural manifestation of God's Spirit today. It is a simple solution to consign these activities to a bygone age. But does such an attitude hold up when brought before Scripture?

These are questions which would rightly require more than a few lines of passing comment. Clearly there are still those claiming to hold a 'dispensationalist' or extreme fundamentalist position who will not recognise charismatics as authentic evangelicals. There are also those committed to a non-evangelical structure who would accept a 'charismatic' label. But these are minority positions. The central position maintained by the vast majority is that the true divide does not lie between 'charismatic' and 'evangelical', but between 'charismatic evangelicals' and 'non-charismatic evangelicals'.

Gavin Reid spoke the mind of many when he wrote on this matter in the *Church of England Newspaper*. He concluded,

The plain fact of the matter is that even the best evangelical religion bears little resemblance to the experience of the Apostles. We have conditioned ourselves not to notice this . . . Is there any good reason why the charismatic element in the New Testament should not continue throughout history? Should we play down evidences of a supernatural

God in case they might disturb the weaker brother? Surely if God is working we should shout it from the housetops. And if our shouting upsets the apple-cart – amen to that!

What is a charismatic?

David Watson used to define the word from its Greek root as meaning 'a recipient of God's grace'. 'Therefore,' he would solemnly announce, 'we are all charismatics.'

Behind that comment lay the basic conviction that we are 'all one in Christ Jesus'. To that sense of basic unity the charismatic movement made four basic contributions:

(a) Evangelical Christianity needs to experience a genuine spiritual renewal within the local church. Correct doctrine or dead textualism is just not enough.

(b) Individuals need to know God in a personal, committed relationship – it is not sufficient just to receive information about him. Being 'filled with the Spirit' (Eph. 5:18) should not be an optional extra but a prime requisite of the spiritual life. Gifts flow in response to God's infilling. Both those which are operated for the benefit of others, along with the gift of tongues which expresses praise to God.

(c) Signs and wonders should be demonstrated again within the Church. God is still a miracle-working God.

(d) A re-emphasis on worship as a joyful, spontaneous and demonstrative expression of love and gratitude to God.

The mere expression of these points of view laid criticism at the door of all that had gone before. One could scarcely expect this to be well received, but a mellowing of attitude has been a distinctive contribution from both sides of the debate in recent years. As non-charismatics have become open to learn, charismatics have acknowledged that they don't possess all the answers.

Charges of fanaticism and of belonging to the 'lunatic fringe' have become less vociferous. In turn charismatics have been open to accept that God works in a variety of ways for each of his children. Many recognise that not everyone

will speak in tongues. The concept of an absolute blueprint
for the spiritual life to which every individual Christian must
adhere, has increasingly been rejected.

As less heat has been generated, so more light has been
thrown on key issues as evangelicals have listened to each
other. The debate is by no means over. Extremes still exist.
But real progress has been made towards genuine reconcilia-
tion and co-operation.

This is most clearly perceived within institutional and
denominational structures. There are now few evangelistic
or missionary societies which would reject candidates simply
because they hold to either a charismatic or non-charismatic
position.

The Fountain Trust of the 1970s brought together leaders
from major evangelical denominations who identified with a
charismatic position. Led in turn by Michael Harper, Tom
Smail and Michael Barling, many were surprised when it
chose to close itself down as a structural entity in 1978. It is
interesting to note that the mantle was not taken up by
inter-denominational bodies. Instead Anglican renewal
ministries and the Baptist and Methodist revival fellowships
along with the Group for Evangelism and Renewal (GEAR)
in the United Reformed Church seemed to fill the breach.

Perhaps even more significant is the way that conservative
evangelicalism, Methodism and the 'Mainstream' Baptist
conference now consciously bridge evangelicals within their
respective denominations. Charismatic and non-charismatic
stand together.

The Pentecostal dilemma

It was in an old mission hall in Azusa Street, Los Angeles.
The year was 1906. People sensed the descent of the Holy
Spirit in a fresh way and expressed their love and devotion to
God in strange tongues.

To a casual observer this would have seemed a suitable
place and date for the origins of the charismatic movement.
But the Pentecostal denominations which were to develop

into such a major force in twentieth-century evangelicalism would perhaps shudder to be called 'the first charismatics'. They owed their origins to Azusa Street and similar outbreaks of spiritual power of the turn of the century. Fifty years later the charismatics appeared on the scene like the bride who had missed out on the wedding!

Outbreaks of miracles and groups engaging in prophecy and speaking in tongues had been an occasional phenomena witnessed throughout 2,000 years of Church history. Rarely had they affected the mainstream of church life. Nor could they be dismissed in a cavalier fashion.

John Wesley wrote,

It does not appear that these extraordinary gifts of the Holy Ghost were common in the church for more than two or three centuries. We seldom hear of them after that fatal period when the Emperor Constantine called himself a Christian . . . From this time they almost totally ceased; very few instances of the kind were found. The cause of this was not . . . 'because there was no more occasion for them' . . . The real cause was, 'the love of many', almost of all Christians, so-called, was 'waxed cold' . . . This was the real cause why the extraordinary gifts of the Holy Ghost were no longer to be found in the Christian Church.

The Pentecostal movement soon appeared in another light entirely. Leaving established churches in frustration, or by expulsion, they formed powerful groupings highly active in evangelism – particularly among the economically deprived sections of the community. If Pentecostalism was a charismatic movement, it was equally a working-class movement committed to evangelism.

The Jefferys brothers' campaigns in the 1920s and 1930s gave the movement a spearhead. The result was three new denominations in Britain: The Assemblies of God (AOG), the Elim Church and the Apostolic Church. To these can now be added a number of primarily ethnic groupings, such as the New Testament Church of God.

The split between the Jefferys brothers and the consequent divide between Elim and AOG caused much heartache. Today the two groups enjoy close relationships, while AOG continues to affirm its commitment to total autonomy for its local assemblies and the belief that the 'baptism in the Holy Spirit' must receive its initial evidence by the recipients speaking in tongues.

Far from existing in isolation the Pentecostal denominations have played an increasingly prominent role in evangelical affairs. Throughout the century they have served continually to remind the evangelical community of the need to recognise the Holy Spirit as a dynamic force in the life of believers. They have retained a commitment to seeing God at work in 'signs and wonders' today. Their emphasis on evangelism in Britain and overseas, along with a wholehearted commitment to Scripture have placed them alongside the Reformed churches and the Brethren as the only denominations to retain a total allegiance to the evangelical tradition. The German Evangelical Alliance still excludes Pentecostals from its membership, but in this country the Rev Eldin Corsie, principal of the Elim Bible College, served for four years as chairman of the British Evangelical Alliance.

To denominations which had taken such a firm stand on these issues, the charismatic movement could easily appear as half-hearted Pentecostals. What is more, this impression was heightened by the reluctance of many charismatics to leave their non-Pentecostal denominations. When others did leave it was generally to form new churches and fellowships outside mainstream Pentecostalism.

It says much for the spiritual maturity of Pentecostal leaders that they have endeavoured to generate links of genuine friendship and fellowship with newer charismatic streams. In recent years non-Pentecostals by denomination, but charismatic by experience, have frequently been given the opportunity to address Pentecostal rallies, conferences and national assemblies.

The house-church movement

Perhaps no four words have more potential to generate heat in evangelical circles than these! This must be a pity, for house-church members are sincere Bible-believing evangelical Christians.

Certainly a great deal of confusion exists over the nature and identity of the house-church movement. For a start, this does not, as the name implies, refer to all who meet in houses instead of halls or church buildings. As some fellowships now number 500 to 1,000 people it would take a very large house to accommodate them!

Many of these fellowships began with small groups which met in homes; the name was acquired – and it stuck! It is, however, doubly misleading. I doubt if there is any such thing as a 'house-church movement'. It is no more than a general title for five or six totally different and fairly unrelated streams of spiritual life and growth (see Appendix 1). They do, however, have certain things in common.

The wave of renewal experienced in mainline denominations through the medium of the charismatic movement is seen as being incomplete. God's purposes in history are viewed as being progressive towards the restoration of church life back to a truly New Testament pattern.

Post-Reformation church history is seen as involving a progressive recovery of biblical perspectives. From sixteenth- and seventeenth-century Lutheran, Presbyterian, Baptist, Quaker and Congregational traditions to eighteenth-century Methodists and Moravians, to the Brethren and Salvation Army in the nineteenth and, finally, in the twentieth century to the Pentecostal, charismatic and ultimately to the Restoration movement (see, *Restoration Magazine*, Nov/Dec, 1983).

Three emphases are clearly identified.
1. Authority–recognised within the church on the Ephesians 4 pattern of 'apostles, prophets, evangelists, pastors and teachers'.

2. Experimentation – as the name of Gerald Coates's team, 'Pioneer', suggests.
3. Discarding – of all that smacks of 'religious institutional-ism' rather than dynamic spiritual life.
Andrew Walker has concluded that

> they are the largest and most significant religious forma-tion to emerge in Great Britain for over half a century. Not since the Pentecostal movements of Elim and the Assemb-lies of God were established in the late 1920s has such a distinctive and indigenous Christian grouping arrived on the religious scene' (*Restoring the Kingdom*, Hodders, 1985).

Their emergence has been heralded by a mass of protest. 'Antinomian', 'pyramid structures', 'authoritarianism', 'new denomination', 'cult', 'brainwashing shepherds', 'sheep stealers' – these and many other jibes have been levelled at their leaders.

The major difficulty lies in the fact that they are not a unified entity. What applies to one group may certainly not apply to another. Different viewpoints, and varied emphases are held by each section. To make matters worse, the emer-gence of hundreds of free evangelical charismatic churches and fellowships owing no allegiance to any Apostle or group has created still greater confusion.

Inevitably the dust will settle. Some extremes will retreat into exclusivism. Perhaps the emergence of a church histo-rian or two will enable them to learn some of the lessons of the Brethren movement on this score. Others will come more into fellowship with fellow-evangelicals without compromis-ing their own distinctives. It is too early to draw sweeping conclusions.

Certainly early accusations of lack of biblical authority, evangelistic zeal, sense of social responsibility and commit-ment to Scripture are generally receding. But the loss of church members, broken friendships, and the sense of rejec-tion which has come with separation will take time to heal. An openness to repair the damage is needed on both sides.

This is true across all the barriers and wounds which men and women have created in these areas of controversy. While some areas of evangelicalism are still struggling with these issues, others are finding support and wisdom as non-charismatic and charismatic share together.

Getting it together

The efforts of men like Gerald Coates, Bob Roxburgh, Keith Munday, Michael Barling, Terry Virgo, Douglas McBain and many others have served to build important bridges. A reciprocal response from non-charismatics is restoring fellowship. Differences are openly discussed and areas of tension progressively resolved.

Difficulties do still exist, but important beginnings have been made. Charismatics still need to pay more attention to the pressures felt by non-charismatics when expected always to respond to a charismatic style of worship meeting. Non-charismatics need to be more open to adjust their traditional responses to learn from their brethren. It is humility and relationships which will make the difference.

Perhaps the last word could be given to Dr Martyn Lloyd-Jones.

> Got it all? Well, if you have got it all I simply ask in the name of God, why are you as you are? If you have got it all, why are you so unlike the New Testament Christians? Got it all! Got it at your conversion! Well, where is it, I ask? ('Quenching the Holy Spirit', *Westminster Record*, September 1969).

Perhaps both sides need to learn from these words.

Whether by seeking to be more sanctified daily, or seeking a continuing onrush of Holy Spirit power, British evangelicals, holding firmly to God's Word, need together to learn from each other what it is daily to be filled by the Holy Spirit. Our family divisions benefit no one but the enemy of our souls.

7

THE NEW EVANGELICALS

This is not a new party. Nor is it a clearly identifiable group; its doctrinal position is classically evangelical. But a tidal wave has hit British evangelicalism in the last twenty years and it is not confined to any one society, denomination or agenda. There is no direct unity apart from shared evangelical conviction. Across the board there exists a new, emergent force of younger evangelicals demanding change in areas of evangelical concern today.

The dynamism of new younger leadership has been significant. Many leaders today are in their thirties or forties, whereas in the 1960s leadership tended to be confined to those in their fifties and sixties. In some senses a revolution has indeed taken place.

This has been largely a 'people movement' rather than a 'clerical movement'. While church structures were seen to have stagnated or fossilised, a desire was vocalised for clear, new initiatives to take place. The result today can be seen in firmly-established new works as diverse as Frontier Youth Trust, Greenbelt, Youth With A Mission, Saltmine Trust, British Youth For Christ, Operation Mobilisation, Care Trust, *Buzz* magazine, Arts Centre Group, In Contact, *Strait* newspaper, Spring Harvest and many others.

Handing on the torch

It has been almost inevitable that older evangelical leaders, and those operating in more traditional areas of activity, should have felt a sense of threat. These new operations did not emerge quietly. Their robust sense of the importance of new tasks carried with it the implication of failure on the part of what had existed before.

Yet, interestingly enough, it was older evangelical leaders who helped to create the climate for change. John Stott, Tom Houston and others were in the vanguard of the Lausanne Movement. The Lausanne Covenant which emerged from the Lausanne Conference of 1974 heralded a new era of evangelical thinking on key issues. Here was a unique twinning of social concerns with evangelistic responsibilities. A denial of the commitment to middle-class morality was coupled with a desire to encourage indigenous, rather than missionary leadership within the so-called Third World. Discipleship and church growth were significant concepts conjoined to the mobilisation of the laity in evangelism.

Meanwhile evangelical theological colleges and Bible training schools were catching on to the new emphases and imparting them to their students. Francis Schaeffer's L'Abri, and later John Stott's London Institute for Contemporary Christianity were in the forefront of developing the concern for Christians to think with a 'Christian mind-set'. No longer was Christian thinking confined to church activities. Now the challenge emerged to focus Christian attitudes and beliefs on all areas of society.

In 1982 Billy Graham was to agree to participate in Mission England, dependent on the active support and agreement of younger leaders. At a special consultation in London they were to agree warmly, but demand that 50 per cent of all organising committees should be composed of people under 40 years of age!

On a personal note I can never forget that in 1980 Luis Palau took me to the United States to work with him over a six-week period. This was in order to give me teaching and training experience in dealing with secular and Christian leaders. Luis had recognised my weaknesses, the older leader was happy to take the younger one under his wing.

Sadly, not all saw their responsibilities in the same light. Many younger leaders were dismissed as mavericks. Others were viewed with concern. Some spoke of 'the angry, rebellious young men and women of British evangelism'. Others saw the problem and yet recognised the potential in younger leaders. In Birmingham the established Anglican leader, David MacInnes, worked in the context of the Jesus Centre with Colin Day and Nick Cuthbert. The twinning of wisdom and maturity with youthful exuberance is always a potential force in developing younger leadership. Sadly, the Birmingham illustration has proved the exception rather than the rule.

It will be interesting to see, in time, how today's younger leaders will either groom or ignore the next generation.

Rock around the church

In the mid-1950s rock hit the world. Ten years later the Church faced the same phenomenon. As young Christians began to sing, first folk songs then amplified folk and on to the formation of rock bands, a new cultural dimension was added to evangelism. At a Brethren assembly in North London a means of contact between all these aspiring communicators was established.

Musical Gospel Outreach (MGO) was founded in the early 1960s. At varying times it operated conferences, music publishing, a management agency and established the major evangelical youth magazine, *Buzz*.

Meanwhile a sleepy Suffolk village awoke to the strident tones of Christian rock presented by All Things New. Those involved were to join with others in founding the annual Christian arts festival, 'Greenbelt'. This unique blend of music, drama, seminars, dance, mime and more music gave a new opportunity for Christians to demonstrate their involvement in 'the arts', and their role in expressing the Christian faith through their art form. A commitment to examine radical social, political, and spiritual perspectives is illustrated, not only in the festival itself, but also through its newspaper, *Strait*.

The early MGO days heralded a procession of groups and

solo artists. A reaction was inevitable. Many have assumed that this was due to the older generation, but in fact younger evangelicals were already voicing their own reservations.

> Today we so easily create our own heroes. A man has an attractive personality, an honest face, he is musically skilled – the next moment he is being moulded by clever, articulate men into becoming a 'superstar' for Jesus. He plays to thousands, his words are treasured, his comments reported, he becomes the apostle of our generation. Yet so often, inside rests a weak frightened personality longing to develop a deeper relationship with God but attracted by the popularity and glamour, manipulated by recording companies or management into pretending to be a spiritual giant (*Sold Out*, Marshalls, 1980).

Too many of the new heroes were gifted musically, but thrust into the limelight without adequate spiritual preparation. High fees, record deals and popular visibility combined with often poor lyrics, spiritual immaturity and expectation of evangelistic results succeeded in bringing frequent disaster. Some went to entertain and were expected to be evangelists. Others wanted to evangelise, only to discover that local Christians had not anticipated that non-Christians would even turn up to their event.

Throughout the 1970s the situation was changing. Well-established artists like Graham Kendrick and John Pantry began to encourage and guide young up-and-coming musicians into developing ministry gifts. British Youth for Christ and Scripture Union provided important opportunities in evangelism, particularly in schools work, for gifted young musicians. Concerts began to involve other means of proclaiming biblical truth. Mime, drama, dance, preaching and even escapology were employed in communicating the Gospel message!

It would be foolish to assume that all early initiatives in Christian contemporary music were fruitless. This would be far from true. Nor would it be correct to suggest that the whole musical subculture has now collapsed and that it would be impossible to attend a Gospel concert without being confronted by a preacher. It would be true to say that there is now far greater understanding and support for Christian musicians. In turn standards have risen and rarely would one now hear a musician attempting a stumbling apology for Jesus. The message has caught up with the medium, as has a recognition of the importance of maintaining the highest spiritual standards in the messenger, too!

Meanwhile, a significant change in direction was taking place – even if the tempo was to remain the same. A rebirth of interest in singing praises to God was to produce a whole new vocabulary of worship. Songs and spiritual 'ditties' were produced by the thousand. Churches learning from groups like the Fisherfolk established their own worship groups of guitarists, piano, and often strings, brass and drums. Major Christian contemporary rock bands now served as musicians to accompany spiritual worship.

This revolution is by no means over! It is, however, showing signs of 'coming of age'. Hymns and even canticles are being introduced. Theological content is maintained as a priority. Closer attention is being paid to accuracy and significance. It must be hoped that this trend continues and that some of the results will be sung in the twenty-first century – alongside the hymns of Charles Wesley and Isaac Watts. Before we just dismiss such thoughts as wishful thinking, it should be remembered that thousands of the hymns of Charles Wesley faded into obscurity – only some stood the test of time and lived on to encourage the Church today.

Mission – new moves

The Church has proved reluctant to relinquish her traditions, but able to absorb innovations. Traditional hymn-books have been joined by either Youth Praise, Psalm Praise, Songs of Fellowship or the Mission England songbook. Rarely has the old been replaced by the new, usually the two exist side by side. The same attitude has applied to missionary concerns as well.

Evangelicals in the nineteenth century had been distinctive for their keen proclamation of biblical truth, for involvement in areas of social concern, but also for enthusiastic hymn singing and bold espousal of missionary initiatives. South-East Asia, the African continent and Latin America had all been the recipients of earnest missionary endeavour. The evangelical missionary societies had grown strong and powerful, but the twentieth century had been a time of swimming against the secularist tide in those nations to which missionaries had once been sent in their hundreds.

Stanley Davies, the general secretary of the Evangelical Missionary Alliance, has helpfully underlined the problems which were faced. At home a crisis of confidence in the Gospel emerged which dampened missionary fervour. The decline of Britain as a political power and the identification of certain by-products of mission with the less-pleasant aspects of colonialism undermined missionary vision. An outdated perspective which viewed the missionary as a jungle-centred 'do-gooder' in khaki shorts, and an ageing missionary-minded constituency did not help the situation. At the same time an overwhelming sense of the spiritual needs of the United Kingdom was contrasted with the growing recognition of incredible church growth overseas.

To face a changing situation in other countries where instability, opposition and church division plagued missionary service, the traditional missionary society began to adapt its role. The balance shifted towards training and developing indigenous, national leadership. The importance of medical and practical skills was emphasised. The priority of translation work was recognised. But recruits were slow to come forward.

More recently the situation has begun to change. A new alliance is emerging between younger networks involved in evangelism in Britain and missionary societies engaged in overseas activities. A new phenomenon has emerged – the short-term missionary. Youth With A Mission (YWAM) and Operation Mobilisation (OM) have been instrumental in popularising the concept of young people giving a few years of their lives to missionary service.

The growth and development of OM and YWAM represent one of the success stories of twentieth-century evangelicalism. Through ships, literature and teams of enthusiastic young people the Christian message is announced around the world.

Older societies have taken hold of the opportunities presented by modern technology. Radio and TV broadcasts, new Bible translations and literature have joined the missionary in reaching hitherto isolated groups of people. Strategic planning and well-practised training and disciplinary methods have become an important part of mission today.

The upsurge of interest in world mission has not been confined to 'new' initiatives. More traditional societies are now beginning to reap the benefits of awakened interest in, and commitment to, the needs of the worldwide Church.

On the continent of Europe a series of mission conferences for young people has served to stimulate further interest. Growing co-operation between older and newer missionary societies, and the fresh input of personnel and ideas from 'charismatic' and 'house churches' are creating new outlooks and encouragement towards mission.

Although there is still a very long way to go – few could have foreseen the beginnings of a radical new awakening of missionary concern in the closing years of the twentieth century. Far from falling off the evangelical agenda, the heightened interest, particularly among the under-thirties, provides a strong indicator that British Christians may again be taking seriously their responsibilities towards mission world wide.

The generation which avidly followed *Tom and Jerry* in the 1960s was to be succeeded by the adherents of Captain Kirk and *Star Trek* in the 1970s. Here was the challenge of uncharted paths and new territories to be won. To go, 'where no one had gone before'!

Gordon Bailey, Philip Vogel and Doug Barnett were among those who pioneered school evangelism. By the end of the seventies it could be claimed that a million unchurched youngsters could hear a rational presentation of the Gospel through school evangelists in Britain each year.

This was not without problems. The classroom is no setting for an evangelistic meeting. But a clear, coherent expression of Christian values and the challenge of Christ began to be expressed thoughtfully. The work of Scripture Union and British Youth For Christ schools workers gained respect as a valuable aid, particularly to Christian teachers.

In universities and colleges, Roger Forster, Michael Green, David Watson, David MacInnes and others were to blaze a trail for evangelism with strong 'apologetic' content. The work of UCCF was to provide an important structure for student involvement in evangelism and mutual encouragement.

In local churches a new emphasis was placed on one-to-one evangelism. The 'Power' programme, One Step Forward campaign, and 'Evangelism Explosion' were to encourage this trend. Coffee bars gave young people both opportunity and training in learning to speak openly to their friends about Jesus. Faith-sharing teams developed; tell-a-tourist campaigns and Jesus festivals gave further opportunities to express the Christian message.

Evangelical roadshows like the 'Fighter' tour, 'Our God Reigns', and 'Let God Speak' drew thousands of people to face messages of challenge to action in today's world. As these developed they were to incorporate a mixture of training, encouragement and information. One message flowed through all these events – passive Christianity was no longer acceptable!

'All change here?'

If you had been brought up in a house overlooking a railway platform, this would not be an unfamiliar cry. But it would

be a very wrong view of contemporary evangelicalism. Much
has, indeed, remained the same.

A visit to All Souls, Langham Place, or to St Helen's,
Bishopsgate, would confirm that little of fundamental importance has changed in recent years. The work of the
London City Mission, UCCF, Crusaders or Christian Col-
porteurs has not undergone an overnight transformation.
Nor should it. Cultural modifications naturally occur – but
there is little need to change a formula that works for those
involved.

This attitude has saved evangelicals from serious division.
Change has come to fit areas of specific need. Change is not
hallowed of itself. Consequently, few younger evangelists
would dare to despise the ministry of senior evangelists, nor
should they. There is plenty of room among evangelicals to
demonstrate unity in diversity and little necessity to feel
threatened by one another.

It is here that a real issue must be faced. Evangelicals do
not always retain the grace to speak well of each other. Those
older in experience can feel 'put down' by the enthusiasm of
younger Christian workers who, in turn, can too easily reject
mature advice. It is at this point that patience must be
exercised, and genuine regard grow from greater contact
with one another.

Contemporary evangelicals still sing hymns and use current worship material. Many are 'charismatic' by experience, but many are not. Some are involved in 'newer'
evangelistic or missionary groupings, others concentrate
their efforts in more traditional networks. Some concentrate
on 'parachurch' involvement, a growing number are more
committed to denominational or independent church patterns. Easy generalisations tend to break down. One fact is
certain and that is a recognition that all have something to
learn from one another.

Perhaps this attitude is the genius of Spring Harvest. In
eight short years this week-long self-styled 'teaching/
training conference in evangelism' rose from an attendance
of 3,000 to over 40,000 people. The teaching programme

focuses around the themes of Scripture, evangelism, social responsibility, world mission and commitment to the local church.

The speaking team at this event will range from Anglican to house–church, charismatic to reformed non-charismatic. Also from younger emerging leaders to senior evangelical statesmen. Its burden is to recover for younger evangelicals a commitment to spiritual discipline, Scriptural authority, missionary zeal and an understanding of their evangelical heritage. Michael Cassidy, the South African Anglican, was to write of his visit to the event,

> We have seen here at Prestatyn a genuine and deep evangelical faith, a commitment to biblical outreach, to evangelism, to social justice, and a sane and powerful experience in renewal of the Holy Spirit. Spring Harvest has been the most perfect mix of these components I have ever seen in all my years of ministry.

Evangelical patterns of ministry have certainly enjoyed a period of broad change and development during the last twenty years. Some have been disturbed by what could easily appear as an over-enthusiastic commitment to cultural trends; others have observed a growing commitment to stay open to changing methods while remaining firmly anchored to the convictions engendered by our evangelical heritage.

8

A BRIGHT TOMORROW?

This brief outline of twentieth-century evangelism will read, to many, as a cautionary tale. And so it is. Division, discord and doubt have all contributed to obscure the testimony of the Gospel. Yet these clouds which remain on the horizon cannot prevent our noticing that change is clearly in the wind! Many evangelicals are recognising that shifts in attitude and recovery of lost direction could point to new beginnings. Indeed, morale is strengthened by an anticipation of the future rarely matched by previous generations.

What, then, are these pointers to change and indications of encouragement? Space allows only a brief mention of each. But when these factors are joined together in the face of contemporary reactions within society they could well point the way towards a very different future for evangelicals in Britain.

Signs of hope

(a) Current statistics serve to convey the picture of numerical growth among evangelicals which is in vivid contrast to other sections of the Church.

(b) Evangelical leaders are emerging into positions of senior responsibility within denominational hierarchies. Several presidents of the Baptist Union and Methodist Conference have been evangelicals. A growing proportion of Anglican bishops are of the same persuasion. Theological colleges record a growing number of evangelical candidates for ordination. These, in turn, render it likely that coming generations will have a higher percentage of evangelicals in positions of strategic importance and able to influence direction in a variety of denominations.

(c) Strategic new evangelistic initiatives are being developed. These place an increasing emphasis on the need for one-on-one evangelism. The stress on the professional evangelist is being accompanied by an underlining of the importance of all being involved in sharing their faith. This is leading to a rapid increase in terms of church growth, congregation building and particularly church planting.

(d) A growing commitment is evident on the part of many to stand against the 'spirit of the age'. This is most clearly seen in a desire to maintain Christian moral standards. We may also be viewing the beginning of a similar concern to fight poverty, injustice, racism and other social issues where individuals suffer. If this were to be coupled with a sense of 'downward mobility' it could result in a return to the rural villages and the inner city and lead to powerful demonstrations of community involvement and 'kingdom living' in a self-seeking world. Sacrifice and cost are involved in the Christian life. Mission at home and abroad is starting to see the fruit of recent re-emphasis on the cost of commitment.

(e) Growing numbers of evangelicals are becoming involved in what formerly appeared to be 'no-go' areas. For instance, politics, local government and the social services. This is accompanied by a re-evaluation of the relative importance of evangelical Christians' being involved in vocational areas such as education, medicine, the police force, and world mission – to name just a few. The development of a variety of evangelical groups working in areas of social and moral concern, along with the rapidly escalating membership of the Evangelical Alliance bear witness to a growing desire among evangelicals to affect the society in which they live. Concern for groups like the victims of famine and disease, the unemployed or mentally handicapped serve to illustrate the essentially practical nature of this contribution. Special support and fellowship groups have been formed to help evangelicals under pressure in professions like the police, probation service, armed forces, media and the arts. All these serve to speak of growing commitment to the community at large.

(f) Once evangelicals appeared to spend most of their time
arguing with each other! Traditionally, these debates re-
sulted in ever-increasing fragmentation. This trend has not
ceased, but a great reversal has taken place in attitudes
towards one another. A growing desire has emerged, particularly among leaders, for dialogue, prayer and cross-
fertilisation of ideas with other evangelicals from different
'tribes' or groupings.

This increased openness to one another is further illustrated by the massive expansion of numbers within evangelical festivals and events which seek to build bridges and
traverse denominational barriers.

(g) A stronger emphasis of fundamental biblical doctrine
and commitment to serious Bible study and prayer is re-
emerging. Small groups of believers meeting together for
prayer, study and discussion have been estimated at above
100,000. Prayer chains, prayer groups and cell groups are
proliferating. Gatherings to 'Pray for the Nation' and the
spread of Bible-study aids provide evidence of growing
momentum.·

This all serves to illustrate how rapidly change is affecting
the evangelical scene. On the one hand the old ghetto-like
mentality of isolation from the world is breaking down; on
the other total separation from fellow evangelicals is becoming a thing of the past as valuable lessons are learned from
cross-pollination with one another.

These processes are not occurring in a vacuum. They take
place against the vivid backdrop of a rapidly changing world.
Nuclear threat, economic fluctuation, and a sense of individual helplessness in the face of the might of the corporate
state, all combine to induce a sense of profound uncertainty.

Rarely has there been a more promising moment to
announce the Christian Gospel – with its twin emphases of
truth and righteousness.

As we face the end of the second millenium since Christ,
the hearts of most people around us are failing them for

fear. It is not the lack of natural resources which is the chief problem, however, but the lack of spiritual and moral resources. Thinking people know that the problems facing us – bewildering in their number, magnitude and complexity – are beyond us. Only a return to the living God who created us, sustains us and can re-make us through Christ, and a recovery of the authentic Christian faith in its biblical fullness and contemporary relevance, can enable us, with confidence and without fear, to look forward to the year 2000 AD (Dr J. R. W. Stott, 'The Year 2000 AD', *London Lectures in Contemporary Christianity*, Marshalls).

But our message has rarely been greeted by the responsive heart of people like the Philippian jailor pleading 'what must I do to be saved?' (Acts 16:30). In general, the Christian message has been ignored.

There are, however, some indications that this is also changing. As evangelical Christians come into conflict with the norms of society, apathy can easily turn to antagonism.

The Early Church historian, Tertullian, once observed that 'the blood of the martyrs is the seed of the church'. Evangelical convictions have always thrived best under pressure or persecution. It could well be that as evangelicalism faces increasing unpopularity a more powerful response will emerge in terms of prayer, witness and holy lives, with signs following.

What is in a name?

Society today hates extreme positions. Everything is reduced to a level of common acceptance. Christianity is fine so long as it remains a club someone can attend, while another goes to a different sort of club – a pub, the British Legion or whatever. In other words, each does his own thing and accepts the actions of others.

A growing militancy in evangelicalism, a desire to assert truth in the face of the growth of modernism, Islam, and spiritism is certain to jar against the mood of our age. To assert that we are right and all others are wrong is bound to provoke a response. To point to Jesus as the only way to God can appear to be blind bigotry. But truth is not relative. Everyone cannot be equally right at one and the same time.

The conviction held by evangelicals that the claims of Jesus Christ are absolute and that Scripture is an adequate foundation to secure that fact has created turmoil both inside and outside the Church.

Many have argued that the Church needs to get its act together. We live within a population which has become thoroughly confused by the meaning of the word 'Christian'. There seem to be so many different viewpoints all claiming that singular label. Some believe the Bible to be true, others do not. Some recognise Jesus as Son of God, others do not. Some deny miracles, others affirm them. No wonder the non-Christian is left enquiring what it is all about?

The easy answer is to settle for the lowest common denominator. Church attendance, baptism as an infant, or even residence in the British Isles are viewed as adequate qualifications for the title 'Christian'.

Within the Church itself the variety persists. Charismatic, Anglican, Fundamentalist, Baptist, Pentecostal, Anglo-Catholic, Modernist – the labels abound! But where does the true significance lie?

Some have argued that each label describes a group acting as a repository for a fragment of the truth. Therefore, the argument for ecumenicism properly understood implies that the whole truth cannot be recovered until all the Churches get together and add their bits and pieces of the truth to one another. On the other hand, evangelicals claim to be a people of the Bible. They claim allegiance to the total revealed word of God and therefore that evangelical theology is biblical theology. Their commitment is to 'the whole counsel of God' (Acts 20:27 RSV).

Dr John Stott has summarised the argument in this way.

It is the contention of evangelicals that they are plain Bible Christians, and that in order to be a biblical Christian it is necessary to be an evangelical Christian. Put that way, it may sound arrogant and exclusive, but this is a sincerely held belief. Certainly it is the desire of evangelicals to be neither more nor less than biblical Christians. Their intention is not to be partisan, that is, they do not cling to certain tenets for the sake of maintaining their identity as a 'party'. On the contrary, they have always expressed their readiness to modify, even abandon, any or all of their cherished beliefs if they can be shown to be unbiblical (*Christ the Controversialist*).

In this firm conviction John Stott goes on to add,

Indeed, since one important meaning of the word 'catholic' is 'loyal to the whole truth', one would dare even to say that, properly understood, the Christian faith, the catholic faith, the biblical faith and the evangelical faith are one and the same thing . . . if evangelical theology is biblical theology, it follows that it is not a new fangled 'ism', a modern brand of Christianity, but an ancient form, indeed the original one. It is New Testament Christianity.

Breaking down the barriers

These words indicate a growing trend. Evangelicals are recovering their nerve – and their morale. They are recovering a sense of confidence in both their roots and their convictions.

The basic evangelical belief in those doctrinal truths is enshrined in the traditional credal statements of the Church. This, coupled with a confidence in Scripture, and the nature of conversion introducing the individual into the realities of a personal relationship with Jesus Christ and the fellowship of the Church, are fundamental to faith. These factors which define an evangelical are being re-emphasised in our day and generation.

It is these convictions that represent, for the evangelical, the sole ground for spiritual unity.

Therefore any marriage between evangelicalism and ecumenicism must be an uncomfortable one. To add the traditions of the Church or the scholarly understanding of man to the revealed will of God in the Bible and to invest them with equal authority is untenable to an evangelical Christian. As Dr Jim Packer has explained,

> You cannot add to evangelical theology without subtraction from it. By augmenting it, you cannot enrich it; you can only impoverish it. Thus, for example, if you add to it a doctrine of human priestly mediation you take away the truth of the perfect adequacy of our Lord's priestly mediation. If you add to it a doctrine of human merit, in whatever form, you take away the truth of the merits of Christ . . . The principle applies at point after point. What is more than evangelical is less than evangelical. Evangelical theology, by its very nature, cannot be supplemented; it can only be denied (*The Theological Challenge to Evangelicalism Today*).

In these uncompromising words the issue is spelled out. Unity is not an issue of sacramental practice or church allegiance but of doctrinal persuasion.

This may scarcely seem like breaking down barriers! Yet once evangelicals appreciate their own position the fear of compromise or absorption into a vast amorphous mass of broad churchmanship recedes. Once we know who we are, and what we believe, we do not need to retreat behind a wall of total isolation. Indeed, we can share truth with others boldly.

This has had dramatic implications for Anglican evangelicals. Far from having to separate themselves from recognition of any role for the sacraments or tradition of the Church, they have been enabled to work out their contribution to faith, but within an evangelical framework. Instead of leaving the Church of England because of the statements of the Bishop of Durham, they have been able to influence the doctrinal response of the House of Bishops and preserve their heritage! This is enshrined for posterity in a resolution carried by both the House of Laity and the House of Clergy to 'confirm belief that the virginal conception and the empty tomb be the faith of the universal church and the Church of England'. Previous statements had given the impression that these were *one* way of expression of the faith of the Church of England – now it is affirmed that they are *the only way*!

Some have discerned twelve different 'tribes' of evangelicals – each with its own distinctives.

Each group tends to develop its own identity, distinctive forms of worship and church government, and eventually adopts or accepts a label which makes it recognisable to everyone else! Within this pattern will emerge structures, doctrinal emphases and recognised leaders. Frequently it is at this point that the clearest illustration of division emerges because key leaders and nationally loved speakers in one 'stream' or 'grouping' will normally be completely unknown outside their own 'constituency'.

Some will bridge the gap through notoriety or reputation gained over many years – but such statesmen are rare.

The variety of evangelical churchmanship is enormous. Evangelicals are discovered in large numbers throughout all the major Protestant denominations. Most new and emerging congregations would appear to be wholeheartedly evangelical. Some smaller denominational groupings like the Pentecostals, Brethren and Strict Baptists have always been totally evangelical in composition and belief.

Some groupings like the Anglican and Baptist evangelicals number hundreds of thousands, while other small groupings of a few thousand proliferate throughout the country. It is also difficult to measure the homogeneity of evangelical groupings. Some are governed by semi-authoritarian structures, others by loose association and others hold to total autonomy within the context of the local congregation. One could spend endless hours contrasting the Church of England Evangelical Council with the Fellowship of Independent Evangelical Churches, a local Strict Baptist Association, the executive council of the Assemblies of God and the 'Bradford House Church' Apostolic team!

Many evangelical believers have chosen to remain in non-evangelical churches. Some have come into a personal commitment to Jesus Christ and chosen to remain in Roman Catholic or Anglo-Catholic churches. It is at this point that genuine difficulties have occurred. Some evangelicals have found it a matter of conscience to 'separate themselves', others have drawn the opposite conclusion.

One might argue that variety is all very well, but how on earth does one manage to get such diverse opinions to act together?

One answer has been to suggest a lowest common denominator to which all should conform. Therefore, if some evangelicals feel uncomfortable in a meeting where hands are raised in the air in worship then that practice should be abandoned by all. If some feel that evangelicals cannot remain in mixed denominations then only those who agree can enjoy true fellowship. This is a means of establishing evangelical unity which has been tried and failed. Our lack of contact with one another at various times in evangelical history bears adequate testimony to that fact.

The other response has been to suggest that those points which divide us are insignificant in the light of all that which holds us together. Surely some can hold to one pattern of worship or style of church government and practise them while releasing others to different forms.

This pattern has led to what some have seen as a very wholesome diversity in evangelical churchmanship. Converts now tend to gravitate to the form of worship and church government within which they feel most comfortable. Choice is clearly the order of the day, although occasioning from time to time uncomfortable tension or confusion as different groups proliferate.

Generally a 'give and take' policy has prevailed. Mutual tolerance and an openness to learn from one another have merged as major signs of hope for the future.

It is too early to claim that a third great evangelical awakening beckons in the closing years of the twentieth century. But there are clear indications of development.

- Evangelical identity is being clearly seen and an evangelical theology is becoming a hallmark of many who would not formerly have identified with such a position.

- Evangelicals in different groups are providing a major influence into the denominations.

- Common concern for the persecuted brethren in other lands is serving to unite many.

- Social responsibility is re-emerging in a position of prominence on the evangelical agenda.

- Evangelism, prayer, Scripture and other positions traditionally held by evangelicals are being reinforced.

These, coupled with a growing desire to learn from each other and make an impact on society with our corporate voice are serving to emphasise our need for unity. Facing a popular front of growing hostility from the world at large, it is becoming clear that evangelicals must make common cause together. This represents an enormous potential within our nation, the opportunity is open to us.

Evangelicals stand at a significant crossroad. One road could lead to gradual disintegration and division into relative obscurity. The other is to emerge into co-operation as a force in this nation, demonstrating what it means to be 'all one in Christ Jesus' and through our combined efforts making again a major impact on our land. We stand, in fact, at a moment for truth to be heard. The sacrificial cost to us may be criticism and non-co-operation; the rewards to the kingdom could be enormous!

If you are considering joining a local evangelical fellowship, starting one, or becoming a member of the Evangelical Alliance in its attempts to represent evangelicals nationally, please write to EA at Whitefield House, 186 Kennington Park Road, London, SE11 4BT.

APPENDIX 1

THE 'HOUSE-CHURCHES'

North
Under the leadership of Pastor Wally North these churches developed initially at the time of 'Henry's Revivals', small, independent fellowships, not related generally to the other streams.

Basingstoke
This group began out of the work of Basingstoke Baptist Church. They now care for a number of churches and fellowships, particularly in the counties of central England. Leaders include Barney Coombes, Peter Hill, Dave Richards, David Church, Tony Gray, and Ron Trudinger.

Chard
This group were early pioneers in the field, establishing a community from which emerged leadership to guide, advise and support local groups. Their best-known leader would probably be Ian Andrews, whose healing ministry has enabled him to cross many barriers within the charismatic constituency.

Independents
Too numerous and diverse to evaluate.

Festival
This group is scarcely homogenous. It revolves around the teams led by Gerald Coates (Pioneer), John Noble (Team Spirit) and David Tomlinson (Team Work) and the work of

Peter Fenwick in Sheffield and beyond. They care for over 180 churches, operate a major week-long event for around 5,000 people (Festival) and support a new missionary enterprise supporting indigenous churches, particularly in Africa (Links International).

Restoration
This grouping seems to be in a state of transition. Bryn and Keri Jones act as apostles to the Bradford stream, which retains a strong degree of exclusivism. There is little direct relating with evangelicals of other streams. This is evidenced in the change of Dales and Wales Bible weeks into a celebration for the involved rather than occasions open to the uninitiated. 'Go' teams, an active programme of church planting, commitment to a satellite-broadcast TV programme and a training college are important parts of their programme.

The two other apostolic teams led by Terry Virgo and Tony Morten give guidance to a large number of churches. They work more readily with other evangelicals. Terry's reformed theological position gave him an interesting opportunity to address the Westminster fellowship. South-West and Downs Bible weeks provide teaching and worship open to those from all church backgrounds. *Restoration Magazine* reflects the views of all three teams.

APPENDIX 2

THE TWELVE TRIBES OF EVANGELICALISM

Clearly any attempt to hone down evangelicals into a limited number of groupings must constitute a simplistic generalisation. However, despite many areas of overlap, these groups exist and may be helpful if we are to understand the basic 'unity in diversity' which does exist in evangelicalism.

1. Anglican evangelicals.
2. Free Churches e.g., Brethren assemblies, independent charismatic churches, etc.
3. Pentecostals.
4. Evangelical *minorities* in mainline denominations (e.g. Methodists, U.R.C., Presbyterians).
5. Reformed and independent separatists (e.g. FIEC, Strict Baptists).
6. Charismatics in 'renewal' sectors of denominations.
7. Parachurch groups.
8. House-churches and independent charismatic churches.
9. Evangelical majorities in denominations (e.g. Baptists, Salvation Army, Free Church of Scotland, etc.).
10. Black churches.
11. Reformed groups in mainline denominations (e.g. Anglicans, Baptists).
12. Missionary churches and groupings.